# SRA Open Court Reading

## Skills Practice

Grade 3

Mc
Graw
Hill
Education

## MHEonline.com

Send all inquiries to:
McGraw-Hill Education
8787 Orion Place
Columbus, OH 43240

ISBN: 978-0-07-667009-3
MHID: 0-07-667009-0

Printed in the United States of America

9 10 LHS 23 22

# Table of Contents

## Unit 4

**Lesson 1**

**Word Analysis** Suffixes -y and -ly . . . . . . . . 1
Latin Suffixes -ment and -ive. . . . . . . . . . . . 3

**Selection Vocabulary** . . . . . . . . . . . 5

**Access Complex Text** Fact and Opinion. . . 7

**Writing** Writing to Inform . . . . . . . . . . . . 9

**Spelling** Suffixes -y and -ly; Latin
Suffixes -ment and -ive . . . . . . . . . . . . . . . 11

**Grammar, Usage, and Mechanics**
Comparative and Superlative Adjectives
and Adverbs . . . . . . . . . . . . . . . . . . . . . . 13

**Lesson 2**

**Word Analysis** Suffixes -ful
and -less . . . . . . . . . . . . . . . . . . . . . . . . 15
Latin Suffixes -able and -ity . . . . . . . . . . . . 17

**Selection Vocabulary** . . . . . . . . . . . 19

**Access Complex Text** Cause and
Effect . . . . . . . . . . . . . . . . . . . . . . . . . . 21

**Writing** Writing to Inform . . . . . . . . . . . 23

**Spelling** Suffixes -ful and -less;
Latin Suffixes -able and -ity . . . . . . . . . . . 25

**Grammar, Usage, and Mechanics**
Abbreviations . . . . . . . . . . . . . . . . . . . . . 27

**Lesson 3 Word Analysis**

Suffixes -ion/-tion/-sion and -al . . . . . . . . . . 29
Multiple-Meaning Words . . . . . . . . . . . . . . 31

**Selection Vocabulary** . . . . . . . . . . . 33

**Access Complex Text**
Compare and Contrast . . . . . . . . . . . . . . . 35

**Writing** Vary How Sentences Begin . . . . . . 37

**Spelling** Suffixes -ion/-tion/-sion and
-al; Multiple-Meaning Words . . . . . . . . . . . 39

**Grammar, Usage, and Mechanics**
Capitalization and Commas—Dates,
Cities and States, Addresses, Titles . . . . . . . 41

**Lesson 4**

**Word Analysis** Suffixes
-ness and -er . . . . . . . . . . . . . . . . . . . . . . 43
Content Words and Words with the
Same Base . . . . . . . . . . . . . . . . . . . . . . . 45

**Selection Vocabulary** . . . . . . . . . . . 47

**Access Complex Text** Classify and
Categorize . . . . . . . . . . . . . . . . . . . . . . . 49

**Writing** Using Multimedia to Illustrate . . . . . 51

**Spelling** Suffixes -ness and -er, Content
Words, and Words with the Same Base . . . . . . 53

**Grammar, Usage, and Mechanics**
Compound Subjects and Predicates . . . . . . . 55

**Lesson 5**

**Word Analysis** Greek Roots
ast, graph, log, and scop . . . . . . . . . . . . . . 57
Latin Roots grat, mar, miss, and port . . . . . . . 59

**Selection Vocabulary** . . . . . . . . . . . 61

**Access Complex Text** Main Idea
and Details . . . . . . . . . . . . . . . . . . . . . . . 63

**Writing** Writing to Explain . . . . . . . . . . . . 65

**Spelling** Greek Roots ast, graph,
log, and scop; Latin Roots grat, mar,
miss, and port . . . . . . . . . . . . . . . . . . . . . 67

**Grammar, Usage, and Mechanics**
Commas in a Series; Commas with
Yes and No . . . . . . . . . . . . . . . . . . . . . . . 69

**Lesson 6**

**Fluency** The Santa Ana Winds. . . . . . . . . . 71
Avalanche! . . . . . . . . . . . . . . . . . . . . . . . 73

**Selection Vocabulary** . . . . . . . . . . . 75

**Access Complex Text**
Making Inferences . . . . . . . . . . . . . . . . . . 77

## Unit 5

**Lesson 1 Word Analysis**

Prefixes re-, pre-, mis-, and un- . . . . . . . . . . 79
Prefixes con- and in-/im- . . . . . . . . . . . . . . 81

**Selection Vocabulary** . . . . . . . . . . . 83

**Access Complex Text** Cause
and Effect . . . . . . . . . . . . . . . . . . . . . . 85

**Writing** Opinion Writing . . . . . . . . . . 87

**Spelling** Prefixes *re-*, *pre-*, *mis-*, *un-*,
*con-*, and *in-/im-* . . . . . . . . . . . . . . 89

**Grammar, Usage, and Mechanics**
Subject/Verb Agreement and Pronoun/
Antecedent Agreement . . . . . . . . . . . 91

**Lesson 2 Word Analysis**
Prefixes *ex-* and *en-/em-* . . . . . . . . . 93
Prefixes *dis-* and *auto-* . . . . . . . . . . . 95

**Selection Vocabulary** . . . . . . . . . . . 97

**Access Complex Text** Main Idea
and Details . . . . . . . . . . . . . . . . . . . . . 99

**Writing** Response to Nonfiction . . . 101

**Spelling** Prefixes *ex-*, *en-/em-*,
*dis-*, and *auto-* . . . . . . . . . . . . . . . . 103

**Grammar, Usage, and Mechanics**
Past, Present, and Future Tense Verbs . . . . . 105

**Lesson 3 Word Analysis**
Number Prefixes . . . . . . . . . . . . . . . 107
Location Prefixes . . . . . . . . . . . . . . . 109

**Selection Vocabulary** . . . . . . . . . . 111

**Access Complex Text** Compare
and Contrast . . . . . . . . . . . . . . . . . . . 113

**Writing** Business Letter . . . . . . . . . . 115

**Spelling** Number Prefixes;
Location Prefixes . . . . . . . . . . . . . . . 117

**Grammar, Usage, and Mechanics**
Irregular Verb Tenses . . . . . . . . . . . . 119

**Lesson 4 Word Analysis**
Words with the Same Base . . . . . . . . 121
Shades of Meaning . . . . . . . . . . . . . . 123

**Selection Vocabulary** . . . . . . . . . . 125

**Access Complex Text**
Classify and Categorize . . . . . . . . . . 127

**Writing** Writing a Summary . . . . . . . 129

**Spelling** Words with the Same Base;
Shades of Meaning . . . . . . . . . . . . . . 131

**Grammar, Usage, and Mechanics**
Prepositions and Prepositional Phrases . . . . 133

**Lesson 5 Word Analysis**
Prefixes and Suffixes . . . . . . . . . . . . 135
Prefixes and Suffixes . . . . . . . . . . . . 137

**Selection Vocabulary** . . . . . . . . . . 139

**Access Complex Text** Sequence . . . . 141

**Writing** Response to Literature . . . . . 143

**Spelling** Prefixes and Suffixes . . . . . 145

**Grammar, Usage, and Mechanics**
Complex Sentences . . . . . . . . . . . . . . 147

**Lesson 6**
**Fluency** The Great Migration . . . . . . . 149
Clothes for the Community . . . . . . . . . 151

**Selection Vocabulary** . . . . . . . . . . 153

**Access Complex Text**
Making Inferences . . . . . . . . . . . . . . . 155

# Unit 6

**Lesson 1 Word Analysis** Compound
Words, Antonyms, and Synonyms . . . . . . . 157
Shades of Meaning, Regular and
Irregular Plurals . . . . . . . . . . . . . . . . . 159

**Selection Vocabulary** . . . . . . . . . . 161

**Access Complex Text** Main Idea
and Details . . . . . . . . . . . . . . . . . . . . . 163

**Writing** Writing a Limerick . . . . . . . . 165

**Spelling** Compound Words, Antonyms
and Synonyms, Shades of Meaning,
Regular and Irregular Plurals . . . . . . . 167

**Grammar, Usage, and Mechanics**
Nouns; Verbs and Verb Phrases;
Subjects and Predicates; Complete
Simple Sentences . . . . . . . . . . . . . . . . 169

**Lesson 2 Word Analysis**
Contractions, Possessives, Irregular Verbs,
and Abstract Nouns . . . . . . . . . . . . . . 171
Homophones, Homographs, and
Multiple-Meaning Words . . . . . . . . . . . 173

**Selection Vocabulary** . . . . . . . . . . 175

**Access Complex Text** Sequence . . . . 177

**Writing** Narrative Writing . . . . . . . . . 179

**Spelling** Contractions, Possessives,
Irregular Verbs, Abstract Nouns,
Homophones, Homographs, and
Multiple-Meaning Words . . . . . . . . . . . 181

**Grammar, Usage, and Mechanics**
Possessive Nouns and Pronouns;
Plural Nouns; Sentence Types;
Subjects and Objects . . . . . . . . . . . . . 183

## Lesson 3 Word Analysis

Inflectional Endings, Regular and Irregular
Comparatives and Superlatives . . . . . . . . . 185

Content Words, Shades of Meaning,
and Words with the Same Base . . . . . . . . . 187

## Selection Vocabulary . . . . . . . . . . . 189

## Access Complex Text Fact and

Opinion . . . . . . . . . . . . . . . . . . . . . . 191

## Writing Response to Literature . . . . . . . . 193

## Spelling Inflectional Endings, Regular and
Irregular Comparatives and Superlatives,
Content Words, Shades of Meaning,
and Words with the Same Base . . . . . . . . 195

## Grammar, Usage, and Mechanics

Pronouns; Abstract Nouns; Conjunctions;
Compound Sentences . . . . . . . . . . . . . . . 197

## Lesson 4 Word Analysis

Suffixes -y, -ly, -ful, -less, -ion/-tion/-sion, -al,
and Latin Suffixes -ment, -ive, -ity, -able . . . . . 199

Multiple-Meaning Words, Suffixes -ness
and -er, Content Words, Words with the
Same Base, and Greek and Latin Roots . . . . 201

## Selection Vocabulary . . . . . . . . . . . 203

## Access Complex Text Cause

and Effect . . . . . . . . . . . . . . . . . . . . . 205

## Writing Biography . . . . . . . . . . . . . . 207

## Spelling Suffixes -ly, -ful, -less,
-ion/-tion/-sion, -ment, -ive, -ity, -able, -ness,
and -er; Content Words; and Greek Roots . . . . 209

## Grammar, Usage, and Mechanics

Adjectives and Adverbs . . . . . . . . . . . . . 211

## Lesson 5 Word Analysis

Prefixes re-, pre-, mis-, un-, con-, in-/im-,
ex-, en-/em-, dis-, and auto-;
Number Prefixes . . . . . . . . . . . . . . . . . . 213

Location Prefixes, Words with the
Same Base, Shades of Meaning, and
Prefixes and Suffixes . . . . . . . . . . . . . . . 215

## Selection Vocabulary . . . . . . . . . . . 217

## Access Complex Text Compare and

Contrast . . . . . . . . . . . . . . . . . . . . . . 219

## Writing Biography . . . . . . . . . . . . . . 221

## Spelling Prefixes re-, pre-, mis-, un-, dis-;
Number Prefixes; Location Prefixes; Suffixes;
Words with the Same Base; and Shades of
Meaning . . . . . . . . . . . . . . . . . . . . . . 223

## Grammar, Usage, and Mechanics

Subject/Verb Agreement; Commas;
Capitalization . . . . . . . . . . . . . . . . . . . 225

## Lesson 6

## Fluency Art for Our Ancestors . . . . . . . . 227

Martha Graham and Modern Dance . . . . . . . 229

## Selection Vocabulary . . . . . . . . . . . 231

## Access Complex Text Classify and

Categorize . . . . . . . . . . . . . . . . . . . . . 233

# Suffixes *-y* and *-ly*

**FOCUS** A **suffix** is a word part added to the end of a base word. The suffix **-y** means "full of" and can be added to some nouns.

- The suffix *-y* changes a noun into an adjective.
  **chill** ("cold") → **a chilly night** (Ex: *a cold night*)
- If the word ends in e, drop the final e before adding *-y*.
  **shad̲e → shad̲y**
- In most cases, double a consonant before adding *-y*.
  **mud → mud̲d̲y**

The suffix **-ly** means "in a certain way" and can be added to some adjectives.

- The suffix *-ly* changes an adjective into an adverb. Remember, an adverb is a word that describes a verb, an adjective, or another adverb.
  **light** ("not heavy") → **skip light̲l̲y** ("skip in a light way")
- If the base word ends in y, change the y to i before adding *-ly*.
  **happ̲y → happ̲i̲l̲y**

**PRACTICE** **Read each *-ly* or *-y* word below. Write the base word on the line.**

1. wildly _____wild_____      5. greasy _____grease_____

2. noisy _____noise_____      6. lucky _____luck_____

3. deeply _____deeply_____    7. necessarily _____necessary_____

4. quietly _____quiet_____    8. foggy _____fogg_____

**APPLY** **Read each sentence below. Complete the definition of the underlined word.**

9. "I won't go!" she said <u>loudly</u>.

   *Loudly* means to do something in a ___noisy___ way.

10. Pat <u>gently</u> picked up the puppy.

    *Gently* means to do something in a ___carful___ way.

11. Dad told the children to clean their <u>dirty</u> room.

    *Dirty* means full of ___trash___ .

12. Clark shook his head <u>sadly</u>.

    *Sadly* means to do something in a ___blue___ way.

13. The old car looked broken and <u>rusty</u>.

    *Rusty* means full of ___rust___ .

14. The <u>needy</u> cat meowed for Dana's attention.

    *Needy* means full of ___Needful___ .

**Read the paragraph below. Find four mistakes the writer made when spelling words with the suffixes -*ly* and -*y*. Cross them out and write the correct spellings above them.**

Recently, scientists studied a ~~sanddy~~ sandy rock. They figured out that this rock used to be part of Mars. It flew ~~quietily~~ quietly through space until it hit Earth. What was important, however, was that this rock had ~~curvey~~ curvy holes in it. On Earth, small living things make holes in rocks. Could there have been life on Mars? It will take years to know if there ~~realy~~ really was life on Mars.

Word Analysis • *Skills Practice 2*

Name _____  Date _____

# Latin Suffixes *-ment* and *-ive*

**FOCUS** The Latin suffix **-ment** can be added to some verbs and means "act of" or "process of."
- The suffix *-ment* turns a verb into a noun.
  **pay** ("to give what is owed") → **pay<u>ment</u>** ("the act of paying")

The Latin suffix **-ive** can be added to some verbs and nouns and means "inclined to" or "likely to."
- The suffix *-ive* turns a verb into an adjective.
  **defend** ("to protect") → **defen<u>sive</u>** ("likely to protect")
- If a base word ends in *e*, drop the *e* and add *-ive*.
  **decorat<u>e</u>** → **decorat<u>ive</u>**
- If a base word ends in *de*, change the *de* to *s* before adding *-ive*.
  **conclu<u>de</u>** → **conclu<u>sive</u>**

**PRACTICE** Read each word with the Latin suffix *-ment* or *-ive* below. Write the base word on the line.

1. retirement _retire_
2. impressive _impress_
3. encouragement _encourage_
4. invasive _invade_
5. employment _employ_
6. narrative _narrate_

*Skills Practice 2* • Word Analysis

UNIT 4 • Lesson 1 **3**

**APPLY** Add the Latin suffix *-ment* to the word in each box below. Write the new word on the line to complete the sentence.

7. | arrange | They made an _arrangement_ to meet after lunch.

8. | entertain | The concert was great _entertainment_.

9. | refresh | We drank apple juice for _refreshment_.

10. | settle | The colonists created a new _settlement_.

11. | achieve | My best _achievement_ is my science award.

Add the Latin suffix *-ive* to the word in each box below. Write the new word on the line to complete the sentence.

12. | persuade | I wrote a _persuasive_ paper on the need to protect wildlife.

13. | create | The story had a very _creative_ plot.

14. | cooperate | The students were _cooperative_ during the fire drill.

15. | innovate | My employer is looking for fresh, _innovative_ ideas.

16. | appreciate | I was very _apprecitive_ of his kindness.

Word Analysis • *Skills Practice 2*

# Vocabulary

> **FOCUS** Review the selection vocabulary words from "The Country Mouse and the City Mouse."

| | |
|---|---|
| **abundance** | **musty** |
| **compost** | **saliva** |
| **craggy** | **scrumptious** |
| **elements** | **scrutinized** |
| **inadequate** | **tone** |
| **luxury** | **tranquility** |

## PRACTICE Circle the vocabulary word that matches each sentence.

**1.** The woman wore an expensive dress and the finest of jewels.

**craggy     inadequate     tranquility     luxury**

**2.** Our baskets were overflowing with berries from the woods.

**inadequate     scrutinized     abundance     musty**

**3.** The wind howled and the rain stung our faces as we walked home.

**elements     scrumptious     luxury     craggy**

**4.** All the boxes that had been in the basement had a strange smell.

**tone     elements     musty     inadequate**

**5.** The lasagna and salad Flora made tasted wonderful.

**tranquility     craggy     compost     scrumptious**

**6.** You will never stay warm in that thin jacket.

**tone     inadequate     luxury     saliva**

**APPLY** Read each sentence and look at the underlined vocabulary word. Answer each question by explaining the definition of the vocabulary word.

7. After my baby sister chewed on the toy, there was <u>saliva</u> on it. What was on the toy? _____

_____

8. Wes loved the <u>tranquility</u> of his favorite spot in the forest. Why did Wes love this place? _____

_____

9. Beth was insulted by the <u>tone</u> Jill used when speaking to her. What was Beth upset about? _____

_____

10. Be careful hiking along the island's <u>craggy</u> coastline. What is this land like? _____

_____

11. Mr. Chang's garden grows well because he uses <u>compost</u>. What does Mr. Chang use? _____

_____

12. Hank <u>scrutinized</u> the document before he signed it. What did Hank do? _____

_____

_____

# Fact and Opinion

> **FOCUS** A **fact** is a true statement that can be proven. An **opinion** is a statement of someone's feelings or beliefs that cannot be proven. Facts and opinions can be expressed by the characters and the narrator in a story.

**PRACTICE** Read each sentence from "The Country Mouse and the City Mouse." Write whether it expresses a fact or an opinion.

1. "What a fabulous idea!" City Mouse said excitedly.

   *opinion*

2. "It sure is quiet and peaceful here," City Mouse remarked.

   *opinion*

3. And what she did sniff did not smell very appealing.

   *opinion*

4. She had collected five seeds, mossy bark from an apple tree, and some musty kernels of corn.

   *fact*

5. "Well, I've never been to the city," Country Mouse said.

   *fact*

6. The dog's teeth snapped shut inches from the pair as they dove into a hole in the wall.

   *fact*

**7.** "I live in luxury," she boasted. "The finest foods are at my fingertips."

_fact_

**8.** Country Mouse searched underneath the hay for food.

_fact_

**APPLY** **Write one other fact and one other opinion expressed by City Mouse and Country Mouse in the story.**

**9.** Page: _14_ Fact from City Mouse: _I live in the city._

**10.** Page: _19_ Opinion from City Mouse: _she live in luxury house._

**11.** Page: _14_ Fact from Country Mouse: _she has really good smell._

**12.** Page: _18_ Opinion from Country Mouse: _It take 4 hours to find food._

**Write one fact and one opinion of your own about living in the country and living in the city.**

**Living in the Country**

**13.** Fact: _there farm animals._

**14.** Opinion: _she think it is qiut the tabe_

**Living in the City**

**15.** Fact: _there is food always food on the table_

**16.** Opinion: _there more food._

# Writing to Inform

## Think

**Audience: *Who*** will read your writing?

_____

**Purpose: *What*** is your reason for writing?

_____

## Prewriting

Use the Venn diagram below to plan your comparing and contrasting text. Write similarities in the overlapping section of the diagram. Then write differences in the outer sections.

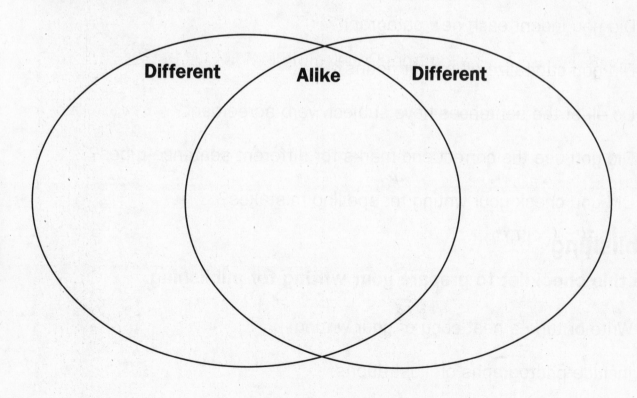

**Different**      **Alike**      **Different**

# Revising

**Use this checklist to revise your writing.**

☐ Did you include compare and contrast signal words?

☐ Did you use transition words to organize your facts and explanations?

☐ Did you include descriptive words and details?

☐ Did you use content words related to your topic?

☐ Did you include a concluding sentence?

☐ Does your writing have a clear purpose?

# Editing/Proofreading

**Use this checklist to correct mistakes in your writing.**

☐ Did you use proofreading symbols when editing?

☐ Did you indent each new paragraph?

☐ Did you capitalize all proper nouns?

☐ Do all of the sentences have subject/verb agreement?

☐ Did you use the correct end marks for different sentence types?

☐ Did you check your writing for spelling mistakes?

# Publishing

**Use this checklist to prepare your writing for publishing.**

☐ Write or type a neat copy of your writing.

☐ Include photographs or illustrations.

# Spelling

> **FOCUS**
> - The suffix **-ly** can change some words into an **adverb**. An adverb is a word that describes a verb, an adjective, or another adverb. If the base word ends in *y,* change the *y* to *i* before adding *-ly.*
> - The suffix **-y** can be added to some nouns to change the noun into an **adjective**. Drop the final e before adding *-y.* You usually double a final consonant before adding *-y.*
> - The suffix *-ment* means "act of" or "process of."
> - The suffix *-ive* means "inclined to" or "likely to."

**Word List**

1. slightly
2. payment
3. partly
4. daily
5. scary
6. chewy
7. inclusive
8. slimy
9. shipment
10. kindly
11. treatment
12. funny
13. grumpy
14. secretive
15. muddy

**Challenge Words**

1. engagement
2. easily
3. sensitive

## PRACTICE Sort the words under the correct heading.

**Change *y* to *i,* add *-ly***

1. _____

2. _____

**Suffix *-ly* without change to base**

3. _____

4. _____

5. _____

## Drop final e, add *-y*

6. _____

7. _____

## Double final consonant, add *-y*

8. _____

9. _____

## Suffix *-y* without change to base

10. _____

11. _____

## Suffix *-ment*

12. _____

13. _____

14. _____

15. _____

## Suffix *-ive*

16. _____

17. _____

18. _____

# Comparative and Superlative Adjectives and Adverbs

**FOCUS**

- **Comparative adjectives** compare two items. They are often formed by adding -er or the word *more*.

  **Examples:** Yesterday was cold*er* than today. Gold is *more expensive* than silver.

- **Superlative adjectives** compare three or more items. They are often formed by adding -est or the word *most*.

  **Examples:** Ryan is the fast*est* runner in our town.

  I saw the *most beautiful* painting at the museum.

- Some comparative and superlative adjectives do not follow these rules. They have special forms.

  **Examples:** I think grapes have a *better* flavor than bananas. Which is the *least* expensive car?

- **Comparative** and **superlative adverbs** compare actions. For short adverbs, add -er and -est.

  **Example:** Ian arrived *latest* of all the guests.

- Use *more* and *most* with adverbs ending in -ly.

  **Example:** I ride my bike *more carefully* now.

**PRACTICE** Read each sentence. Write *Adj.* if the sentence contains a comparative or superlative adjective and *Adv.* if it contains a comparative or superlative adverb.

1. You mom is the most generous person I know. _Adj_

2. Jacob jumped higher than Gavin. _Adv_

3. Ken played the most skillfully and won the contest. _Adv_

4. Your outfit is more colorful than mine. _Adj_

**APPLY** Read each sentence. Circle the correct form of the superlative or comparative adjective or adverb.

5. The (most pretty, (prettiest)) dress was the one Trinity wore.

6. My parents arrived (more early, (earlier)) than Luis's parents.

7. The tree house was ((sturdier,) more sturdily) built than the shed.

8. Let's buy the (softer, (softest)) towels the store sells.

9. Imani is the (cheerfuller, (most cheerful)) person I've ever met.

Write a sentence using each adjective or adverb. Use the comparative or superlative form, as indicated in parentheses.

10. happy (comparative) _City mouse is happier living in the city than country mouse._

11. slowly (comparative) _I slowly walked to school._

12. thoughtful (superlative) _Sidney is the most thoughtful frend I have._

13. safely (superlative) _My mom is the safest person I know._

14. straight (superlative) _My dad is the straight person every._

Grammar • *Skills Practice 2*

# Vocabulary

> **FOCUS** Review the selection vocabulary words from
> "A Saguaro's Story."

| | |
|---|---|
| bold | frantic |
| challenge | nourish |
| collapsed | resided |
| cooperate | simple |
| crisis | stage |
| devour | support |

## PRACTICE Write each vocabulary word next to its synonym.

**1.** feed _____

**2.** fearless _____

**3.** gobble _____

**4.** failed _____

**5.** lived _____

**6.** easy _____

**7.** work together _____

**8.** step _____

**9.** assist _____

**10.** emergency _____

**11.** dare _____

**12.** panicked _____

**APPLY** Read each sentence. Use the underlined clues to select the vocabulary word that best completes each sentence. Write the word in the blank.

**13.** The mother bird will _____ her young by <u>feeding them</u> the worms she has gathered.

**14.** These math problems are quite _____; they are so <u>easy</u>, in fact, that I will be finished in only a few minutes.

**15.** We really should try harder to _____ because <u>working together</u> will help us build the playground quickly.

**16.** Avi _____ in New York when he was little, but now he <u>lives</u> in Vermont.

**17.** Grace was a _____ leader who <u>had the courage</u> to speak up for her group.

**18.** Andi was _____ when she couldn't find her little brother; she was so <u>wild with fear</u> that she ran up and down the street shouting his name.

**19.** When Brett decides to _____ me to a race, I can never tell whether he is serious about his <u>call to compete</u>.

**20.** The children are so hungry they will probably _____ the sandwiches and <u>eat</u> the soup <u>with great energy</u>.

# Cause and Effect

**FOCUS** Remember that a **cause** is the reason why
something happens, and an **effect** is what
happens as a result. Finding causes and effects
in a story can help you understand how story
events are related. Look for signal words, such
as *because, since, therefore,* and *so,* to help you
identify cause-and-effect relationships.

**PRACTICE** **Read each sentence. Write *Cause* if the
underlined part describes a cause. Write *Effect* if it
describes an effect.**

**1.** <u>The ice is melting</u> because the freezer is broken.

Effet

**2.** <u>Mr. Rivera is running late,</u> so class will not start for another five minutes.

Cause

**3.** Since <u>Tessa hates cold weather,</u> she will not join us on the skiing trip.

_____

**4.** Avery has a sore throat, so <u>Kaya will be singing the solo tonight.</u>

_____

**_APPLY_ Read the sentences below. Draw a line to match each cause from "A Saguaro's Story" with its effect.**

| Causes | Effects |
| --- | --- |
| 5. The water within the cactus is drying up. | a. Birds began to build homes in the saguaro. |
| 6. As it grew, the saguaro drew more water from the ground. | b. The red-tailed hawk becomes frantic. |
| 7. The saguaro grew arms. | c. The saguaro's fruit drops to the desert floor. |
| 8. The red-tailed hawk leaves her nest to hunt. | d. A great horned owl takes over a nest in the saguaro. |
| 9. The red-tailed hawk sees an owl in her nest. | e. The cactus is shrinking. |
| 10. The birds shake the saguaro by flapping their wings. | f. The palo verde tree died. |

**Each sentence below describes a cause. Think of a possible effect. Then write a new sentence that expresses the cause-and-effect relationship.**

11. Isobel has been crying all morning. _____

_____

12. The flowers hadn't been watered all week. _____

_____

Access Complex Text • **_Skills Practice 2_**

# Writing to Inform

## Think

**Audience:** *Who* will read your research report?

_____

**Purpose:** *What* is your reason for writing a research report?

_____

## Prewriting

**Use the graphic organizer below to brainstorm questions you could answer about your topic in a research report.**

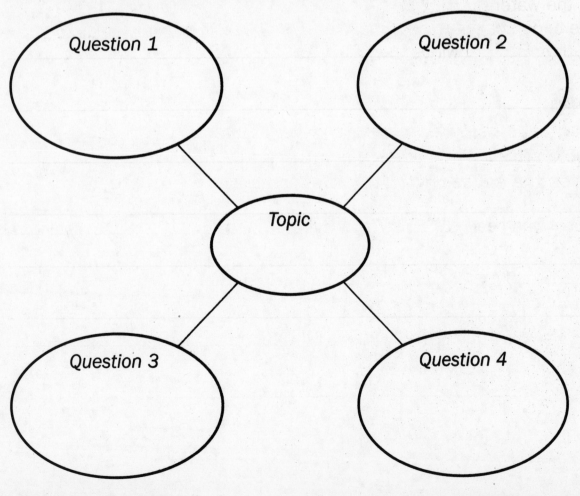

Question 1

Question 2

Topic

Question 3

Question 4

**PRACTICE** Use the lines below to take notes from the following paragraphs.

Manatees are gentle creatures. They quietly float along and munch on sea grass. The way manatees graze has earned them the nickname "sea cows." Manatees travel in herds like cows, too.

Manatees live in the warm, shallow water of marshes. West Indian manatees are found in the Gulf of Mexico and the Caribbean Sea. They are the manatees most people are familiar with. Some manatees also live in the coastal waters of Africa and in parts of the Amazon River in South America.

Manatees are mammals. They live in the water, but they do not have gills. They must rise to the surface periodically to breathe air. While they are submerged, they can close their nostrils to keep the water out. This also keeps the air inside. By filling their huge lungs with air, manatees can float easily through the water.

_____

_____

_____

_____

_____

_____

# Spelling

## FOCUS

- The suffix **-ful** means "full of."
- The suffix **-less** means "without."
- The suffix **-ity** means "state of being."
- The suffix **-able** means "able or tending to be."

When adding suffixes, for words ending in:

- final e, drop the e before adding the ending.
- final y, change the y to i before adding the ending.

**Word List**

1. sleepless
2. painful
3. fixable
4. rarity
5. helpful
6. endless
7. sanity
8. wishful
9. notable
10. penniless
11. wearable
12. activity
13. careless
14. harmful
15. likable

**Challenge Words**

1. plentiful
2. breathless
3. electricity

## PRACTICE Sort the spelling words under the correct heading.

**Change -y to i, add -ful**

1. _____

**Suffix -ful without change to base**

2. _____

3. _____

4. _____

5. _____

## Drop e, add -able

6. _____

7. _____

## Suffix -able without change to base

8. _____

9. _____

## Change -y to i, add -less

10. _____

## Suffix -less without change to base

11. _____

12. _____

13. _____

14. _____

## Drop e, add -ity

15. _____

16. _____

17. _____

## Suffix -ity without change to base

18. _____

# Abbreviations

**FOCUS**
- An **abbreviation** is a shortened form of a word or phrase. Many abbreviations end with periods.

  **Examples:** department = dept.    yard = yd.

- Abbreviations for proper nouns are capitalized.

  **Examples:** Mister Jones = Mr. Jones
  United States = U.S.

- Some abbreviations, especially for the names of businesses and organizations, do not use periods when each letter stands for a word.

  **Examples:** digital video disc = DVD
  North Atlantic Treaty Organization
  = NATO

**PRACTICE** For each word, circle the correct abbreviation.

1. street
   **a.** stre.   **b.** st.   **c.** strt.

2. October
   **a.** Oct.   **b.** Octob.   **c.** otbr.

3. quart
   **a.** quar.   **b.** qt.   **c.** quart.

4. Junior
   **a.** Jun.   **b.** Jnor.   **c.** Jr.

5. feet
   **a.** ft.   **b.** fet.   **c.** f.

6. Mount
   **a.** Mnt.   **b.** Mt.   **c.** Mont.

7. compact disc
   **a.** C.D.   **b.** cd   **c.** CD

8. population
   **a.** pop.   **b.** popul.   **c.** ppln.

**APPLY** Read each sentence. On the line, write the full form of the word or words that are abbreviated.

9. The desk is 50 in. long. _inches_

10. Bob Gordon Sr. is the head of the company. _Senior_

11. If you are holding ticket no. 43, please come forward. _number_

12. The library is on Pecan Ave., near the school. _Avenue_

13. On Jan. 12, we will have a day off from school. _January_

14. Drive along N. Wilson Road until you see the sign. _North_

15. Pablo Picasso (b. 1881, d. 1973) was perhaps the greatest artist of the 20th century. _born_ _died_

**Write a sentence using the abbreviation for each word or phrase in parentheses.**

16. (miles per hour) _mph. MPH_

_____

17. (Street) _St._

_____

18. (December) _Dec._

_____

19. (National Aeronautics and Space Administration) _____
_NASA_

20. (Mister) _Mr._

_____

# Multiple-Meaning Words

> **FOCUS** **Multiple-meaning words** are words that share the
> same spelling but have different meanings. They
> may or may not have different pronunciations.
> Use a dictionary to determine if a word is a
> multiple-meaning word.
>
> Example: ***conduct***
> conduct (kən dukt')          conduct (kon' dəkt)
> "to lead or direct"          "how a person
>                                behaves"

**PRACTICE** Read each sentence. Circle the correct
definition for the underlined word based on the context of
the sentence.

1. My favorite <u>state</u> to visit is Colorado.
   **a.** to express in speech or writing   **b.** a territory within a country

2. The workers went on <u>strike</u> after their pay was reduced.
   **a.** a protest organized           **b.** to hit one's body part
   by employees                         against something

3. Jamie, the babysitter, will <u>watch</u> us while our parents go out for the
   evening.
   **a.** to care for                   **b.** a timepiece worn on the wrist

4. Kamal turned <u>right</u> onto Fallingwell Street.
   **a.** true or correct               **b.** a direction; the opposite of left

5. The toddler shrieked in delight as she was pushed on the <u>swing</u>.
   **a.** to cause to move back         **b.** a movable seat found on a
   and forth                            playground

6. During math class, we learned about a new <u>figure</u> called an octagon.
   **a.** a shape, such as              **b.** a person's bodily shape
   a triangle or square

**APPLY** Read the riddles below. Write the word from the word box that answers each riddle. Each word will be used twice.

| | | |
|---|---|---|
| minor | patient | pitcher |

**7.** I am calm and forgiving. What am I? _____

**8.** I can be used for making and pouring lemonade. What am I?
_____

**9.** I am not very important or valuable. What am I? _____

**10.** My goal is to strike out the batter. What am I? _____

**11.** You will find me in a doctor's office, as sick as can be.
What am I? _____

**12.** I am under the age of eighteen. What am I? _____

**Read each sentence. Write a definition for each underlined multiple-meaning word based on the context of the sentence.**

**13.** Sentence 1: Dahlia began to <u>mold</u> the clay for her art project.

_____

Sentence 2: Mom said, "Clean the bathroom to keep <u>mold</u> from growing."

_____

**14.** Sentence 1: Ms. Langley will <u>train</u> her dance team for the competition.

_____

Sentence 2: The line of cars waited five minutes for the <u>train</u> to go by.

_____

**32** UNIT 4 • Lesson 3

Word Analysis • *Skills Practice 2*

# Vocabulary

> **_FOCUS_** Review the selection vocabulary words from "Einstein Anderson and the Mighty Ants."

| | |
|---|---|
| corporation | harness |
| economy | schemes |
| exoskeletons | technology |

**_PRACTICE_** **Read each sentence and look at the underlined vocabulary word. Circle _True_ or _False_ to show whether the vocabulary word is used correctly.**

**1.** You could <u>harness</u> the power of a horse to help you pull a cart.

   **True**        **False**

**2.** An <u>economy</u> is a system in which goods and services are exchanged for money.

   **True**        **False**

**3.** <u>Schemes</u> are what you would pack for a journey or trip.

   **True**        **False**

**4.** A <u>corporation</u> usually has a president and employees, or workers.

   **True**        **False**

**5.** Bears and moose have <u>exoskeletons</u>.

   **True**        **False**

**6.** You don't need current knowledge or skills to create new <u>technology</u>.

   **True**        **False**

**APPLY Complete the following sentences. Make sure you show the meaning of the underlined vocabulary word.**

7. One of the schemes I have come up with is _____

_____

_____

8. At the science fair, we saw several examples of new technology, such as _____

_____

_____

9. The mill will harness the power of the rushing waterfall to _____

_____

_____

10. Eli is learning about America's economy, or its system _____

_____

_____

11. Mia's aunt is the vice president of a corporation that _____

_____

_____

12. The exoskeletons of ants and other insects are important because

_____

_____

# Vary How Sentences Begin

**FOCUS**  Sentences that all begin the same way can sound boring. Here are some tips for varying your sentence beginnings.

- Begin with an adverb: <u>Hopefully</u> you can come to my party.
- Begin with an adjective: <u>Sad</u> about missing the party, I went to bed early.
- Begin with a time or order word: <u>Now</u> it is time to eat cake!

**PRACTICE**  **Read the following paragraph. Then use the hints listed below to rewrite some of the sentences.**

Sarah could not sleep. Sarah got out of bed. Sarah walked across the room in the dark. Sarah opened her window. Sarah looked out and saw the moon. The moon was full.

**1.** Change the beginning of a sentence. Use a pronoun instead of a noun.

_____

**2.** Change the beginning of a sentence. Add a time or order word.

_____

**3.** Change the order of the words in a sentence.

_____

**4.** Change the beginning of a sentence. Use an adverb.

_____

# Proofreading Symbols

¶     Indent the paragraph.

^     Add something.

℘     Take out something.

/     Make a small letter.

≡     Make a capital letter.

sp     Check spelling.

⊙     Add a period.

# Spelling

> ## *FOCUS*
> - The suffix **-ion/-tion/-sion** means "action of" or "process of." If a word ends in *t*, add *-ion*. If a word ends in *te*, drop the *te* and add *-tion*. If a word ends in *se*, drop the *se* and add *-sion*.
> - The suffix **-al** means "relating to."
> - **Multiple-meaning words**, or homographs, are words with the same spelling but different meanings. Sometimes the words have different pronunciations as well.

**Word List**

1. normal
2. tension
3. scale
4. eruption
5. lead
6. comical
7. vacation
8. present
9. second
10. criminal
11. match
12. reaction
13. content
14. coastal
15. pollution

**Challenge Words**

1. entrance
2. survival
3. explosion

## *PRACTICE* Sort the spelling words under the correct heading.

**Add *-ion* to base word**

1. _____

2. _____

**Drop *te*, add *-tion***

3. _____

4. _____

## Drop se, add -sion

5. _____

## Drop de, add -sion

6. _____

## Suffix -al

7. _____

8. _____

9. _____

10. _____

11. _____

## Homographs with same pronunciations

12. _____

13. _____

14. _____

## Homographs with different pronunciations

15. _____

16. _____

17. _____

18. _____

# Capitalization and Commas—Dates, Cities and States, Addresses, Titles

**Focus**
- Capitalize the names of cities, states, and countries. Place a comma between the name of a city and the state or country where it is located.

  **Examples:** El Paso, Texas    Paris, France

- Capitalize each part of a street name.

  **Examples:** West Fourth Avenue    Old Post Rd.

- For an address within a sentence, place a comma between the street address and the name of the city as well as between the city and state.

  **Example:** We live at 765 North Avenue, Austin, Texas 78710.

- Capitalize names of days and months. Place a comma between the day and the month. Place a comma before the year if it is included.

  **Example:** I will graduate on Tuesday, May 24, 2016.

- Capitalize the first word, last word, and all important words in the title of a book.

  **Example:** *Where the Sidewalk Ends*

**PRACTICE** Write *C* if the sentence has correct capitalization and punctuation. Write *I* if the sentence is incorrect.

1. The mayor will speak to our class on Friday February 17. _____

2. Nadia is moving to Lansing, Michigan. _____

3. The police department is located at 45 East Trade Street, Chicago Illinois, 60603. _____

4. The most popular book in my class is *horton hears a Who!* _____

## APPLY Read each sentence. Add commas where they are needed. Draw three lines under letters that should be capitalized.

5. The board meeting will be postponed until wednesday november 16 2016.

6. Our school's address is 2345 new hope road phoenix arizona 85010.

7. Have you ever read *on the banks of plum creek?*

## Write a sentence with each of the following:

8. an address _____

_____

9. a date _____

_____

10. a book title _____

_____

Grammar • *Skills Practice 2*

# Suffixes -ness and -er

**FOCUS** A **suffix** is a word part added to the end of a base word. The suffix **-ness** can be added to some adjectives and means "state of being."

- The suffix -*ness* changes a word—usually an adjective—into a noun.

  **dark** ("having no light") → **dark<u>ness</u>** ("the state of having no light")

- If the base word ends in *y*, change the *y* to *i* before adding -*ness*.

  **empty** → **empt<u>iness</u>**

The suffix **-er** can be added to some verbs and means "someone or something who" does something.

- The suffix -*er* changes a verb into a noun.

  **lead** ("to guide") → **lead<u>er</u>** ("one who helps to guide other people")

- If the base word ends in *e*, drop the e and add -*er*.

  **manag<u>e</u>** → **manag<u>er</u>**

**PRACTICE** Read each word with the suffix -*ness* or -*er* below. Write the base word on the line.

1. computer _Compute_
2. craziness _crazy_
3. quickness _quick_
4. bowler _bow_
5. massiveness _massive_
6. reporter _report_
7. mixer _mix_
8. sickness _sick_

**APPLY** Read each sentence below. The definition of each missing word is shown in parentheses. Complete the sentence by writing the correct word with the suffix *-ness* or *-er* on the line.

9. Some people think the ___bitterness___ of lemons tastes unpleasant. ("the state of being bitter")

10. Gemma loves the ___freshness___ of clean sheets on her bed. ("the state of being fresh")

11. The company hired a ___designer___ to create its new website. ("one who designs")

12. Our campfire glowed in the ___darkness___ as we sat and told stories. ("the state of being dark")

13. Marissa asked for ___forgiveness___ after she broke the vase. ("the state of forgiving")

14. Ernest Shackleton was an ___explorer___ who made three trips to Antarctica in the early 1900s. ("one who explores")

15. My older brother is learning to become a ___driver___. ("one who drives")

16. The extreme ___brightness___ of the lights gave me a headache. ("the state of being bright")

17. Tania works as an ___interpreter___ at the Japanese embassy. ("one who interprets")

18. A ___catcher___ sends signals to the pitcher. ("one who catches")

# Content Words and Words with the Same Base

> **FOCUS** • **Content words** are specific to a topic or a subject area. They provide meanings and examples as a way of better understanding a given topic or subject area.
> **Example:** A *squall* is "a sudden, violent storm." Therefore, *squall* is a content word related to *weather*.
>
> • **Words with the same base** belong to a family of words. When you add a prefix or suffix (or both) to a base word, the word's meaning changes. Sometimes, the part of speech changes as well.
> **Example:** Base word → *complete*
> Words with the same base as *complete* → *completely, incomplete, completion*

**PRACTICE** Read each set of words. Circle the content word in each set that is related to the topic of weather.

1. banker    (cyclone)    vacation    lifeguard

2. hospital    emergency    (meteorologist)    radio

**Circle the words that belong to the same word family in each row. Then write the base word on the line.**

3. (reuse)    uncle    (misuse)      *use*

4. (agreement)   (disagree)   meeting    *agree*

5. (preparation)   (unprepared)   (preparedness)   *prepare*

**APPLY** Read each sentence below. Then read the definition for the missing content word located under each sentence. Write a word from the word box to complete each sentence.

| seasons | precipitation | forecast | fog |
|---------|---------------|----------|-----|

**6.** Rainforests get more _____fog_____ than most other ecosystems.

"water that falls to the ground in the form of rain, snow, or sleet"

**7.** There are four _____seasons_____: winter, spring, summer, and autumn.

"specific time periods during a year marked by different patterns of weather"

**8.** It was very hard to see through the dense _____forecast_____.

"particles of water floating near ground level, which creates a hazy effect"

**9.** The weather _____precipitation_____ indicates lots of sun and warm temperatures for the next five days.

"a prediction made about the weather after studying given data and information"

**Read each sentence. Change the underlined word to a word from the same word family that makes sense in the sentence. Write the new word on the line.**

**10.** Mr. Ackerman is teaching us _divide_ rules. _____divided_____

**11.** The story's surprise ending was _expected_. _____unexpected_____

**12.** The _settle_ came to America seeking new opportunities and religious freedom. _____settles_____

**13.** Karla _wise_ followed her aunt's good advice. _____unwise_____

**14.** He _save_ only important documents and threw out the others. _____saved_____

**15.** We read the _direct_ on the side of the box. _____direction_____

Name _____  Date _____

# Vocabulary

> **FOCUS** Review the selection vocabulary words from "Amazing Animals."

| advantage | terrain |
|---|---|
| defenses | tolerate |
| lure | ward off |

**PRACTICE** Read each sentence. Replace the underlined word or phrase with the appropriate vocabulary word in parentheses. Write the vocabulary word on the line.

**1.** One of the <u>protections</u> that kept soldiers safe in the past was the fort. **(terrain, lure, defenses)** _____

**2.** In order to <u>attract</u> more customers to her lemonade stand, Brittany lowered her price. **(lure, ward off, tolerate)**

_____

**3.** Nick did not think he could <u>put up with</u> such hot weather for much longer. **(lure, advantage, tolerate)**

_____

**4.** Jamie has an <u>edge</u> over all the other piano players because she has long fingers. **(defenses, terrain, advantage)**

_____

**5.** We must find a way to <u>keep away</u> all the ants that have been sneaking into the kitchen. **(ward off, advantage, terrain)**

_____

**6.** The <u>land</u> of a desert is very different from that of a northern pine forest. **(lure, tolerate, terrain)** _____

Copyright © McGraw-Hill Education

## APPLY Read each question. Write your answer as a complete sentence.

**7.** Do many animals in the wild need to have defenses? Why or why not?

_____

_____

**8.** When you are hiking, does the terrain affect what kind of shoes you wear? Why or why not?

_____

_____

**9.** Would you want to ward off a cold or the flu? Why or why not?

_____

_____

**10.** Could you tolerate a longer school day? Why or why not?

_____

_____

**11.** Do businesses want to lure good and talented workers? Why or why not?

_____

_____

**12.** Does great speed give one animal an advantage over others? Why or why not?

_____

_____

# Classify and Categorize

**FOCUS** Remember that classifying the information in a text can help you understand and remember it. When you **classify**, you sort objects or ideas into **categories**. Categories name groups of things that are related in some way.

**PRACTICE** Classify the items in the box. Write each one under the correct category.

| oak | ocean | bakery | pine | sculpture | lake |
|-----|-------|--------|------|-----------|------|
| bank | painting | maple | mosaic | restaurant | pond |

**1. Forms of Art**

painting

mosaic

sculpture

**2. Bodies of Water**

lake

pond

ocean

**3. Kinds of Trees**

oak

pine

maple

**4. Types of Businesses**

restaurant

bank

bakery

**APPLY** The animals listed in the box are mentioned or shown in "Amazing Animals." Classify these animals by writing them under the correct habitat.

| | | |
|---|---|---|
| zebra | octopus | anglerfish |
| wood frog | camel | giraffe |

**5.** Live on Land

camel

zebra

giraffe

**6.** Live on or Near Water

wood frog

octopus

anglerfish

Think of other categories you could use to classify animals. Then think of animals you could list under those categories. Write the categories and animals below.

**7.** Category: home pet

**8.** Animals: cat

lizerd

dog

**9.** Category: on land

**10.** Animals: camel

zebra

giraffe

**11.** Category: fuzzy

**12.** Animals: Lion

tiger

dog

**13.** Category: in water

**14.** Animals: octopus

anglerfish

shark

# Using Multimedia to Illustrate

## Planning

**Brainstorm ideas for using multimedia sources to illustrate your research report. Record your ideas in the cluster web below.**

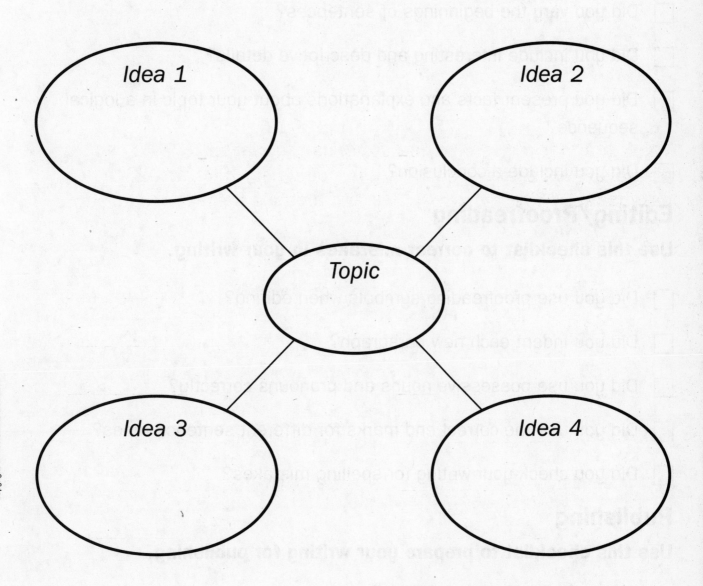

# Revising

**Use this checklist to revise your writing.**

- [ ] Did you include a strong opening with an informative topic sentence?

- [ ] Did you include context clues to help readers understand new words?

- [ ] Did you use time and order words to connect ideas and organize the information?

- [ ] Did you vary the beginnings of sentences?

- [ ] Did you include interesting and descriptive details?

- [ ] Did you present facts and explanations about your topic in a logical sequence?

- [ ] Did you include a conclusion?

# Editing/Proofreading

**Use this checklist to correct mistakes in your writing.**

- [ ] Did you use proofreading symbols when editing?

- [ ] Did you indent each new paragraph?

- [ ] Did you use possessive nouns and pronouns correctly?

- [ ] Did you use the correct end marks for different sentence types?

- [ ] Did you check your writing for spelling mistakes?

# Publishing

**Use this checklist to prepare your writing for publishing.**

- [ ] Write or type a neat copy of your writing.

- [ ] Use a multimedia source to add an illustration or other visual element.

# Spelling

**FOCUS**
- The suffix **-ness** means "state of being."
- The suffix **-er** means "one who" or "something that."
- **Content words** have specific meanings related to the subject of a text. For example, an article about basketball might have the following content words: *hoop, foul line, layup, referee.*
- Words sometimes share the **same base word**. Adding inflectional endings, prefixes, or suffixes to the base word can change its meaning. For example, the words *coloring, colorful,* and *discolor* all share the same base word: *color.*

**Word List**
1. weakness
2. moved
3. manager
4. nation
5. moving
6. trumpeter
7. fitness
8. movement
9. zipper
10. equator
11. blindness
12. remove
13. fairness
14. continent
15. swimmer

**Challenge Words**
1. elevation
2. unhappiness
3. photographer

**PRACTICE** Sort the spelling words under the correct heading.

**Words with the same base**

1. _____

2. _____

3. _____

4. _____

## Suffix -ness

5. _____

6. _____

7. _____

8. _____

9. _____

## Suffix -er

10. _____

11. _____

12. _____

13. _____

14. _____

## Content words related to the subject of world geography

15. _____

16. _____

17. _____

18. _____

**Name** _____ **Date** _____

# Compound Subjects and Predicates

**FOCUS**
- The **subject** names who or what a sentence is about. A **simple subject** is the main word or words in a sentence.
  My <u>mother</u> is a doctor.

- A **compound subject** has two or more simple subjects combined by a conjunction.
  <u>Jonah</u> and <u>I</u> went horseback riding.

- The **predicate** tells what the subject is or does. A **simple predicate** tells one thing about the subject.
  My sister <u>visits</u> her best friend.

- A **compound predicate** tells two or more things about the same subject. They are connected by a conjunction.
  The zebras <u>eat</u> and <u>sleep</u> at the zoo.

**PRACTICE** Read each sentence. If the underlined words are two simple subjects, write **S**. If they form a compound subject, write **C**.

1. <u>Abraham Lincoln</u> was born in 1809, and <u>he</u> first lived in Kentucky. ___S___

2. Then <u>he</u> lived in Illinois, and <u>he</u> got married. ___S___

3. <u>Lincoln</u> and his <u>wife</u> moved when he became president. ___C___

**Read each sentence. If the underlined words are two simple predicates, write S. If they form a compound predicate, write C.**

**4.** Lincoln <u>read</u> and <u>thought</u>, and then he wrote many speeches.

_____ C _____

**5.** He <u>helped</u> slaves because he <u>thought</u> everyone should be free.

_____ C _____

**6.** The North <u>fought</u> and <u>won</u> the Civil War, and slavery ended.

_____ C _____

**_APPLY_ Read the following paragraphs. Circle compound subjects, and underline compound predicates.**

A large number of Germans moved to Cincinnati in the 1800s. Most of these immigrants did not have much, and they wanted better lives. They lived and worked near a waterway. The Germans called it "the Rhine" because they remembered the Rhine River in their homeland. The waterway and nearby area were called Over-the-Rhine.

Few workers could afford to buy a house, so they worked and saved together. Friends and neighbors put some money in a pot every week. Then they drew straws. Whoever picked the right straw got all the money. That person and his family could then buy a house.

# Latin Roots *grat, mar, miss,* and *port*

---

**FOCUS** **Roots** are word parts that have meaning. Knowing **Latin roots** can help you understand new words.

- The root **grat** means "pleasing." It is used in words such as <u>grat</u>eful.
- The root **mar** means "sea." It is used in words such as <u>mar</u>itime.
- The root **miss** means "send." It is used in words such as dis<u>miss</u>.
- The root **port** means "carry." It is used in words such as <u>port</u>able.

---

**PRACTICE** **Read each word and its meaning. Underline the Latin root in the word. Then write the root's meaning.**

**1. congratulated** ("to have told people you are happy for them")

_____

**2. transport** ("to move something from one place to another")

_____

**3. mission** ("a special job a person is sent to finish") _____

**4. marine** ("relating to the sea") _____

**5. support** ("to help") _____

**6. marina** ("a small harbor for boats") _____

**APPLY** **Use words from the previous page to complete each sentence below.**

**7.** In 1998, a spacecraft was sent to _____ cameras and other machines to Mars.

**8.** The spacecraft's _____ was to find out about the history of water on Mars.

**9.** If Mars once had water, then it might have had _____ bacteria. These are small things that live in water.

**10.** People back on Earth worked to _____ the mission and guide the spacecraft.

**11.** Other scientists _____ these people for their good work.

**Use three of the words from the previous page in sentences of your own.**

**12.** _____

_____

**13.** _____

_____

**14.** _____

_____

Word Analysis • *Skills Practice 2*

# Vocabulary

> **FOCUS** Review the selection vocabulary words from "Ecosystem Invaders."

| | |
|---|---|
| **belong** | **fragrant** |
| **carry** | **level** |
| **cling** | **mussel** |
| **effect** | **ornamental** |
| **Eurasian** | **root** |
| **flex** | **tame** |

**PRACTICE** Write the vocabulary word that matches each clue below.

**1.** a bottle of perfume _____

**2.** show a bicep, or arm muscle _____

**3.** the opposite of a cause _____

**4.** a lion in a circus _____

**5.** each stage in a video game _____

**6.** member of a club _____

**7.** a clam-like creature _____

**8.** an insect spreads disease _____

**9.** a baby holding on to its mother _____

**10.** fancy wood carving on a front door _____

## APPLY Read each statement below. Rewrite the sentence using a vocabulary word.

**11.** A certain kind of shellfish has been an invasive species in Lake Erie.

_____

**12.** A pig uses its snout to dig around in the mud.

_____

**13.** When you tighten one muscle, another muscle is often stretched out.

_____

**14.** The Ural Mountains are a land feature located where Europe and Asia meet.

_____

**15.** Some features on the outside of a car are only for decoration.

_____

**16.** Herbs such as basil and thyme are tasty and have a nice aroma.

_____

**17.** The law resulted in a positive change in working conditions.

_____

**18.** The skateboard park is not a place for small children to play.

_____

**Name** _____ **Date** _____

# Main Idea and Details

---

***FOCUS*** Remember that the **main idea** of a paragraph
or selection is the most important overall point
that the author wants to make. The sentence
in a paragraph that expresses the main idea is
called the **topic sentence**. An author supports the
main idea with **details**, which can include facts,
descriptions, explanations, or definitions.

---

***PRACTICE*** **Read the paragraph. Write the main idea
and the supporting details on the lines.**

   A peaceful brook runs through the meadow. Cute lambs and calves
run around in the field. I can pick sweet, juicy apples in the orchard. And
the hayloft is perfect for hide-and-seek. My grandma's farm has it all!

**1.** Main Idea: _____

**2.** Supporting Detail: _____

_____

**3.** Supporting Detail: _____

_____

**4.** Supporting Detail: _____

_____

**5.** Supporting Detail: _____

_____

**APPLY** Read the following paragraphs from "Ecosystem Invaders." Write whether the underlined sentence contains the main idea or a supporting detail.

6. <u>The feral, or wild, pig is not like the tame animals you can find on farms.</u> Spanish explorer Hernando de Soto first brought pigs to North America in 1539. Many farmers let their pigs run free over the years. As a result, some of the pigs ran away to live in the wild.

_____

7. Zebra mussels damage an ecosystem because they eat so much. They eat tiny water plants called plankton. <u>Native species also eat plankton.</u> The native species starve when the zebra mussels eat so much of their food source.

_____

**Read the topic sentence below. Write four more sentences that give supporting details.**

8. People travel for many reasons.

_____

_____

_____

_____

_____

_____

Access Complex Text • *Skills Practice 2*

# Writing to Explain

## Think

**Audience: Who** will read your explanatory writing?

_____

_____

**Purpose: What** is your reason for your explanatory writing?

_____

_____

## Prewriting

**Use this graphic organizer to identify the topic of your explanatory writing. Then list three cause-and-effect relationships that you will include in your writing.**

| Topic |
|-------|
|       |

| Cause | | Effect |
|-------|---|--------|
|       | → |        |

| Cause | | Effect |
|-------|---|--------|
|       | → |        |

| Cause | | Effect |
|-------|---|--------|
|       | → |        |

# Revising

## Use this checklist to revise your writing.

☐ Did you include a topic sentence that clearly identifies your subject?

☐ Did you use sequence signal words and cause-and-effect signal words?

☐ Are there details or descriptions you could add to help make your explanatory writing clearer?

☐ Does your writing communicate a clear purpose?

# Editing/Proofreading

## Use this checklist to correct mistakes in your writing.

☐ Did you use proofreading symbols when editing?

☐ Did you use plural nouns correctly?

☐ Do all of your sentences have subjects and predicates?

☐ Is every word and special term spelled correctly?

☐ Does every sentence end with the correct punctuation mark?

# Publishing

## Use this checklist to prepare your writing for publishing.

☐ Write or type a neat copy of your writing.

☐ Use digital tools to produce or publish your writing.

# Spelling

> **FOCUS** Roots are word parts that have certain meanings. These roots come from the Latin language:
> - The root **grat** means "thankful or pleasing."
> - The root **mar** means "sea or ocean."
> - The root **miss** means "send."
> - The root **port** means "carry."
>
> These roots come from the Greek language:
> - The root **ast** means "star."
> - The root **graph** means "write."
> - The root **log** (sometimes spelled *logue*) means "word" or "study."
> - The root **scop** means "see."

**Word List**
1. congratulate
2. mission
3. report
4. autograph
5. astronaut
6. dialogue
7. import
8. marine
9. photograph
10. mariner
11. dismiss
12. gratitude
13. astronomy
14. apology
15. telescope

**Challenge Words**
1. biography
2. microscope
3. transportation

# PRACTICE Sort the spelling words under the correct heading.

## Latin root *grat*

1. _____

2. _____

## Latin root *mar*

3. _____

4. _____

## Latin root *miss*

5. _____

6. _____

## Latin root *port*

7. _____

8. _____

9. _____

## Greek root *ast*

10. _____

11. _____

## Greek root *graph*

12. _____

13. _____

14. _____

## Greek root *log*

15. _____

16. _____

## Greek root *scop*

17. _____

18. _____

# The Santa Ana Winds

Southern California erupted into flames in the fall of 2003. Twelve devastating wildfires began across the area. In all, the fires burned an area the size of Rhode Island. Wildfires are nothing new to California residents. However, the fires in the fall of 2003 were among the worst to ever occur in the region.

How did the fires spread so rapidly? The fierce Santa Ana winds were one of the causes. The Santa Ana winds are strong, hot, dry winds. They blow from the east or northeast during the fall and winter in Southern California. The winds created ideal conditions for an inferno.

The Santa Ana winds begin high in the mountains along California's eastern border. They commonly reach speeds of thirty miles per hour. Sometimes they gust to over 100 miles per hour!

Besides fanning the flames of wildfires, the Santa Anas have other effects. The most obvious effect is hot, dry weather. The winds lower the humidity and raise temperatures. During the Santa Anas, plants, animals, and people all need more water.

Allergy sufferers also dread the arrival of the Santa Anas. In Southern California, the wind usually comes from the west. This Pacific Ocean breeze is fresh, cool, and free of dust and pollen. But the Santa Anas blow from the east. They carry pollen from the deserts. They stir up dust. This makes life difficult for people who have to cope with allergy symptoms.

The Santa Anas do have some positive effects, though. Surfers eagerly await the winds. As waves come in from the west, the Santa Anas slow them down by blowing from the east. This creates tall waves for surfers to ride. It also gives surfers a longer ride. Divers like the winds, too. The winds bring about clean, clear water. This results in excellent viewing of sea life below the surface.

The winds are helpful to some animals. The clear water that divers enjoy also benefits sea life. It allows algae to bloom and enrich the food chain. Fish, birds, and even whales enjoy this abundance of food.

Monarch butterflies spend spring and summer in the mountains. When the Santa Anas begin, these beautiful insects begin to migrate. They ride the winds on their westward journey.

The Santa Ana winds are well known in California. Weather reports warn of their arrival. Although many people dislike the winds, they will continue to blow. They will fan wildfires, irritate allergies, and create hot weather. But most people will choose to live with them rather than leave an area they have grown to love.

**Name** _____ **Date** _____

# Avalanche!

Avalanches—powerful snow slides—occur on snowy mountains. In the United States, most avalanches occur on the tall mountains of the West.

You might see a small version of an avalanche on a slanted house roof. The snow may become too heavy and slide off. Or warmth from the sun may melt the snow a little and cause it to slide off. Mountain avalanches are similar, but they are dangerous. When snow begins sweeping down a mountain, it can take large rocks and trees with it. And as snow piles up quickly in winter, the risk becomes greater.

The steepness, or slope, of a mountain is important when it comes to avalanches. If a mountain is too steep, snow will not build up. It will slide off continually. If a mountain is not steep enough, snow will not slide at all. But if a mountain has just the right slope, dangerous avalanches can be common.

Each snowfall adds a new layer of snow to these slopes. Over time, the snow compresses down. The strong snow layers are thick and solid. The weak ones are fluffy and loose. If a strong layer builds up on a weak one, the snowpack becomes unstable. The weak layer caves in. This can be the start of an avalanche.

Any sudden weather change can trigger an avalanche. If snow falls very quickly, the existing snowpack does not have time to adjust to the new weight. The sudden increase in weight can trigger a slide.

Rain or a sudden rise in temperature can also do it. If the snow starts to melt, it becomes wet. Wet snow is not very stable. It is likely to slide.

*Skills Practice 2* • Fluency

UNIT 4 • Lesson 6 **73**

Wind is also a problem. Wind can blow snow into large mounds quickly. The rapid weight change caused by the wind can trigger an avalanche.

Although weather can cause avalanches, people are most often the cause. Skiers, climbers, and snowboarders can set off avalanches. They can also get caught in those avalanches.

Luckily there are avalanche experts. They check the snowpack and study the weather. They dig holes in the snow to examine the layers. They can tell if an avalanche is likely to occur. They advise people about unsafe areas. Sometimes they even cause an avalanche on purpose.

Controlled avalanches take place near ski areas, roads, and railroads. People leave the area. Then experts use explosives to start a slide. The idea is to set it off before it falls on its own.

There is no way to prevent avalanches, but thanks to these experts, they can hopefully be avoided.

# Vocabulary

> **FOCUS** Review the selection vocabulary words from "Is This Panama?"

| chemical | routes |
|----------|--------|
| landed | ruins |
| ominous | scoop |
| organ | strange |
| probe | undercoat |
| reproduce | vast |

**PRACTICE** Circle the correct word to complete each sentence.

1. A (chemical/organ) change happens when rust forms on metal.

2. Dark clouds might seem (probe/ominous) to sailors at sea.

3. We explored the (ruins/undercoat) of an old castle in England.

4. If animal species cannot (strange/reproduce), they will become extinct.

5. It is hard to imagine just how (scoop/vast) the Pacific Ocean is.

6. The largest (organ/ruins) of the human body is skin.

7. Some northern birds have an (ominous/undercoat) to keep them warm.

8. A snowy day in Hawaii would be very (vast/strange).

9. Use a spoon to (probe/scoop) the sour cream out of the carton.

10. This spaceship has been designed to (reproduce/probe) the surface of Mars.

11. Check the map for different (ruins/routes) we can take to Atlanta.

12. Tara's plane (landed/routes) more than an hour ago.

**APPLY** Read the clues below. Write the vocabulary word that best fits each clue.

13. I am a heart that pumps blood throughout the body.

_____

14. I am short feathers or fur beneath a top layer.

_____

15. I am something that remains from ancient times.

_____

16. I am something you see in an atlas, or book of maps.

_____

17. I describe a large expanse of land, such as a continent.

_____

18. I am something a bird did when it stopped flying.

_____

19. I describe a feeling of bad luck to come.

_____

20. I am something that all living things do.

_____

# Making Inferences

> **FOCUS** Remember to **make inferences** about the characters, settings, or events in a story as you read. When you make an inference, you understand something that is not directly stated by the author. To do this, consider what you already know along with certain details from the text.

**PRACTICE Read the paragraph and answer the questions that follow.**

Nala had been walking the trails for what seemed like hours. *Every path looks the same,* she said to herself with a frown. *Why didn't I bring a map?* Suddenly, Nala noticed that the light was beginning to fade and the sun was going down. She became slightly lightheaded with a rising panic.

**1.** What does the writer tell you in these sentences?

_____

_____

_____

_____

**2.** Based on what you know, what kind of situation would cause the feelings Nala is having?

_____

**3.** What inference can you make about Nala's situation?

_____

**APPLY** Read each passage from *Is This Panama?* Answer the questions that follow to make an inference.

Sammy spotted a ptarmigan. All summer the ptarmigans had been hard to see because their brown feathers blended in so well with the landscape. Lately, though, their brown feathers were being replaced by white ones.

4. What kind of weather happens in the North during winter? What does the landscape look like? _____

_____

5. Using this knowledge, what inference can you make about why the ptarmigan's feathers are turning white? _____

_____

A couple of nights later, Sammy was surprised to see stars glittering below him.

"Those aren't real stars," a black-throated green warned. "Just try to ignore them."

6. What kinds of light might a bird see below him while flying at night?

_____

_____

7. What does the black-throated green say about the "stars" Sammy sees?

_____

_____

8. What inference can you make about what the "stars" are?

_____

_____

# Prefixes *re-*, *pre-*, *mis-*, and *un-*

> ## *FOCUS*  A **prefix** is a word part added to the beginning of a base word or root.
> - The prefix **re-** means "again."
>   **build** ("to form with materials") → **rebuild** ("to form with materials again")
> - The prefix **pre-** means "before."
>   **bake** ("to cook in an oven") → **prebake** ("to cook in an oven ahead of time")
> - The prefix **mis-** means "wrongly" or "badly."
>   **judge** ("to form an opinion about") → **misjudge** ("to form the wrong opinion about")
> - The prefix **un-** means "the opposite of."
>   **fold** ("to lay one part over another") → **unfold** ("to take one part off of another")

## *PRACTICE*  Read each definition below. Use the prefix *re-*, *pre-*, *mis-*, or *un-* to write a word that matches each definition.

1. "to behave badly" _misbehave_

2. "to locate again" _relocate_

3. "made ahead of time" _premade_

4. "to do the opposite of pack" _unpack_

5. "to consider again" _reconsider_

6. "to treat wrongly" _mistreat_

**APPLY** Combine the prefix *re-*, *pre-*, *mis-*, or *un-* with each base word below. Write the new word and its meaning on the line.

| Prefix | Word | New Word/New Meaning |
|---|---|---|
| 7. *pre-* | game | pregame – before the game |
| 8. *mis-* | information | misinformation – wrong information |
| 9. *re-* | learn | relearn – learn agin |
| 10. *un-* | known | unknown – not know |
| 11. *pre-* | order | preorder – order before |
| 12. *mis-* | understand | misunderstand – understand incorrectly |
| 13. *re-* | fuel | refuel – to full agin |
| 14. *un-* | usual | unusual – to be differnt |

**Choose two words from the Practice activity or the activity above. Write a sentence using each word.**

15. My friend had to relearn how to walk.

16. I miserstand how to do the stuff

Word Analysis • *Skills Practice 2*

# Prefixes *con-* and *in-/im-*

**FOCUS** A **prefix** is a word part added to the beginning of a base word or root.

- The prefix **con-** means "with" or "together." Usually, this prefix is not added to a base word that can stand alone.
  **conference** ("a formal meeting in which people come together for discussion")

- The prefix **in-/im-** means "not."
  **firm** ("solid") → **infirm** ("not solid")
  **proper** ("appropriate") → **improper** ("not appropriate")

**PRACTICE** Add the prefix *con-* or *in-/im-* to the given base word or root to form a word from the word box. Then write the new word on the line.

| inhumane | condense | informal | connect | immobile |
|---|---|---|---|---|

| Prefix | | Base Word/Root | New Word |
|---|---|---|---|
| **1.** _____ | + | formal | _____ |
| **2.** _____ | + | mobile | _____ |
| **3.** _____ | + | dense | _____ |
| **4.** _____ | + | humane | _____ |
| **5.** _____ | + | nect | _____ |

**APPLY** Read each sentence. Write a word from the word box to complete the sentence.

| insignificant | conform | impersonal | conspired |
|---|---|---|---|

**6.** The criminals _____ to commit an illegal act.

**7.** While I think the new scientific findings are important, my friend thinks they are _____.

**8.** Some people believe that sending an electronic thank-you note is _____.

**9.** In order to start a new club at school, we must agree to _____ to certain rules.

## Read each sentence and the words below it. Circle the word that correctly completes the sentence.

**10.** Chris is becoming very _____ with his dog because it constantly chews his shoes.

    **a.** impatient         **b.** consensus

**11.** It is unkind to be _____ of people who are different from you.

    **a.** condense         **b.** intolerant

**12.** My doctor wants me to _____ with a specialist about my broken ankle.

    **a.** insecure         **b.** consult

Word Analysis • *Skills Practice 2*

# Vocabulary

> **FOCUS** Review the selection vocabulary words from "The Road to Democracy."

| | |
|---|---|
| colonists | peaceful |
| documents | region |
| election | revolution |
| empire | trend |
| government | unity |
| nation | vote |

**PRACTICE** Write each vocabulary word next to its synonym.

**1.** papers _____

**2.** settlers _____

**3.** area _____

**4.** style _____

**5.** choice _____

**6.** country _____

**7.** calm _____

**8.** ruling group _____

**9.** togetherness _____

**10.** rebellion _____

**11.** decision _____

**12.** realm _____

# APPLY Complete the following sentences. Be sure to show the meaning of the underlined vocabulary word.

13. One <u>trend</u> my friends and I follow is _____

_____

14. On the day of the <u>election</u> for class president, _____

_____

15. When Rachel wants to visit a <u>peaceful</u> place, she goes to _____

_____

16. To show their <u>unity</u>, the teammates _____

_____

17. The American settlers started a <u>revolution</u> because _____

_____

18. If Sara had gotten one more <u>vote</u>, _____

_____

19. One <u>nation</u> that is close to the United States is _____

_____

20. The king hoped that his <u>empire</u> would someday _____

_____

Vocabulary • *Skills Practice 2*

# Cause and Effect

**FOCUS** Remember that a **cause** is the reason why something happens, and the **effect** is what happens as a result. Look for signal words, such as *because, since, therefore,* and *so,* that will help you identify cause-and-effect relationships.

**PRACTICE** **Read each sentence. Draw one line under the cause. Draw two lines under the effect.**

1. School is closed Monday because it is a national holiday.

2. Since Riley is the fastest runner, he will go last in the relay race.

3. Steve wanted to learn how to sew, so he asked his grandmother for help.

4. All the icicles melted because the sun shone all afternoon.

5. Because the polar bear is white, it blends in with its snowy surroundings.

6. Julie just turned eighteen; therefore, she can register to vote.

7. Kara is shy, so she is usually afraid to meet new people.

8. Since Trey loves animals, he wants to become a veterinarian.

9. We cannot see the moon since it is a cloudy night.

10. Jack's neighbors were angry because his dog kept digging in their garden.

**APPLY** Read each sentence. Write either the cause or the effect described in the sentence.

**11.** When Brett planted the tree in better soil, it began to grow quickly.

Cause: _____

**12.** Olivia is unhappy because her best friend is moving away.

Effect: _____

**13.** The beach is closed today because of the dangerous surf.

Effect: _____

**14.** We didn't read the instructions, so we didn't assemble the toy correctly.

Cause: _____

**15.** If this rain doesn't stop, the streets will be flooded by noon.

Effect: _____

**Read these sentences from "The Road to Democracy." Write whether the underlined words describe a cause or an effect.**

**16.** <u>With the end of slavery</u>, millions of African-American men gained the right to vote.

_____

**17.** And as democracy spreads, <u>the world has become safer and more connected</u>.

_____

**18.** Throughout much of history, leaders gave up their power only <u>when they were forced to do it</u>.

_____

Access Complex Text • *Skills Practice 2*

# Opinion Writing

## Think

**Audience: Who** will read your opinion writing?

_____

**Purpose: What** is your reason for writing about your opinion?

_____

## Prewriting

**Think of reasons that will persuade others to agree with your opinion. Evaluate each idea, and choose the three reasons that will most likely persuade your audience.**

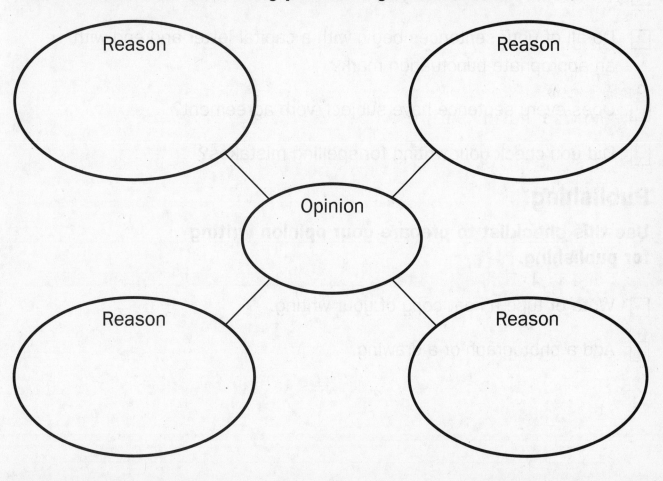

# Revising

**Use this checklist to revise your opinion writing.**

☐ Does your writing state an opinion?

☐ Did you support your opinion with reasons that will appeal to your audience?

☐ Did you use transition words?

☐ Is it clear that your purpose is to persuade?

☐ Did you use language that is appropriate for your audience?

# Editing/Proofreading

**Use this checklist to correct mistakes in your opinion writing.**

☐ Did you use proofreading symbols when editing?

☐ Do all of your sentences begin with a capital letter and end with an appropriate punctuation mark?

☐ Does every sentence have subject/verb agreement?

☐ Did you check your writing for spelling mistakes?

# Publishing

**Use this checklist to prepare your opinion writing for publishing.**

☐ Write or type a neat copy of your writing.

☐ Add a photograph or a drawing.

# Spelling

**FOCUS** A word changes meaning when a prefix is added to the beginning of the word.
- The prefix *re-* means "again" or "back."
- The prefix *pre-* means "before."
- The prefix *mis-* means "wrong" or "bad."
- The prefix *un-* means "not" or "opposite of."
- The prefix *con-* means "with" or "together."
- The prefix *in-/im-* means "not" or "opposite of."

**Word List**

1. mismatch
2. unclear
3. reread
4. unzip
5. concur
6. incorrect
7. unload
8. pretest
9. restart
10. misplace
11. confide
12. impolite
13. prefix
14. unfair
15. improper

**Challenge Words**

1. impossible
2. preschool
3. inexpensive

**PRACTICE** Sort the spelling words under the correct heading.

**Prefix *re-***

1. restart
2. reread

**Prefix *im-***

3. impossible
4. improper
5. impolite

**Prefix pre-**

6. prefix

7. preschool

8. pretest

**Prefix mis-**

9. mismatch

10. misplace

**Prefix con-**

11. concur

12. confide

**Prefix in-**

13. incorrect

14. inexpensive

**Prefix un-**

15. unzip

16. unfair

17. unload

18. unclear

# Prefixes *ex-* and *en-/em-*

**FOCUS** A **prefix** is a word part added to the beginning of a base word or root.
- The prefix **ex-** means "out."
  **export** ("to send out goods or products to another country for sale")
- The prefix **en-/em-** means "put into or onto" or "to cause to be."
  **large → enlarge** ("to cause to be bigger")

**PRACTICE** Read each sentence and set of answer choices. Circle the word that correctly completes the sentence. Then write the word on the line.

1. I do not want my pets ___exposed___ to the extreme heat, so I will keep them inside.
   **a.** engaged          **b.** exposed

2. I was ___embarrassed___ by my mismatched shoes and socks.
   **a.** expended          **b.** embarrassed

3. The city planner did not want to ___endanger___ visitors; therefore, hazardous areas of the park were blocked off.
   **a.** endanger          **b.** embrace

4. A team of scientists will ___explore___ a remote area of Easter Island, located in the southeast Pacific Ocean.
   **a.** entwine          **b.** explore

**APPLY** Read each sentence below. Choose a word from
the word box to complete the sentence.

| extinguisher | employer | ensure | exchange |

5. We will _____ensure_____ that the doors are locked when
we leave the house.

6. In case of an emergency, adults should know where the fire
_____extinguish_____ is located and how to use it.

7. Thad plans to _____exchange_____ his new shirt for one that
is the correct size.

8. Marla's _____employer_____ promoted her to a new position.

**Write a short paragraph using at least four words with prefixes
from either the Practice activity or the activity above. Circle the
words, and make sure they are spelled and used correctly.**

_____

_____

_____

_____

_____

_____

Word Analysis • *Skills Practice 2*

# Prefixes *dis-* and *auto-*

> ***FOCUS*** A **prefix** is a word part added to the beginning of a base word or root.
> - The prefix ***dis-*** means "not" or "the opposite of."
>   **agree** ("to have the same opinion") → **disagree** ("to not have the same opinion")
> - The prefix ***auto-*** means "self."
>   **biography** ("a person's life story") → **auto**biography ("a biography that is self-written")

***PRACTICE*** **Read each word below. Circle the base word. Think about the meaning of the prefix and the base word, then write the word's meaning.**

**1.** disadvantage _____

**2.** disbelieve _____

**3.** dishonest _____

**4.** displease _____

**Draw a line to match each word below with its meaning.**

**5.** autograph      **a.** my life's story written by me

**6.** autopilot      **b.** a self-powered machine with wheels that people use to drive themselves places

**7.** automobile      **c.** a program that allows a ship or spacecraft to steer on its own

**8.** autobiography      **d.** someone's self-written name

## APPLY Complete each sentence below with a word from the box.

| | | | |
|---|---|---|---|
| dishonest | dislikes | autobiography | disagreed |
| discovered | disinterested | autograph | autopilot |

9. Katharine Hepburn, a famous actress, wrote an

_____ called *My Life*.

10. After listening to the lecture for an hour, many people became bored

and _____.

11. The brothers _____ over who was the better
basketball player.

12. A _____ person cannot be trusted.

13. Most modern aircraft are equipped with _____.

14. While walking along the beach, I _____ a sand
dollar that had washed ashore.

15. Tracy _____ roller coasters because she is
afraid of heights.

16. I was able to get the author to _____ my
favorite book!

# Main Idea and Details

> ***FOCUS*** Remember that the **main idea** of a paragraph or selection is the most important overall point that the author makes. The sentence in a paragraph that expresses the main idea is called the **topic sentence**. The author supports the main idea with **details**.

***PRACTICE*** Read each paragraph from "Every Vote Counts." Draw two lines under the topic sentence. Draw one line under each supporting detail.

1. Voters need to learn as much as they can about the candidates before they vote. They can read articles in the newspaper or online. They can listen to the candidates speak. Voters look for the candidates whose views are closest to their own.

2. The Democratic and Republican parties are the two largest political parties, but they are not the only ones. Every election, candidates from other parties, often referred to as third party candidates, run for office. While no third party candidate has been elected president, many have been elected to prominent positions like senator or state governor.

3. After citizens have cast their vote and polling places have closed, the votes are counted. This can take some time, depending on how close the election is. In the election of 2000, it took 36 days for the votes to be counted and recounted! It was a close race between Al Gore and George Bush. Bush was finally declared the winner.

**APPLY** Read each topic sentence below. Write three sentences that provide supporting details.

**4.** I see many things on my way to school in the morning.

I see cars.

I see a bus

I see a house.

**5.** Summer is the best time of the year.

I like to go to the beach.

there no school.

I like popsices.

**6.** Eve decided to make breakfast for her family.

She made pancakes.

She made eggs.

She made juice.

**7.** There are a number of fun ways to get more exercise.

You can run.

**8.** That is the ugliest dog I have ever seen!

# Response to Nonfiction

**Audience: Who** will read your response to nonfiction?

_____

**Purpose: What** is your reason for writing?

_____

## Prewriting

Use the Venn diagram below to compare and contrast information from the text. Write similarities in the overlapping section of the diagram. Then write differences in the outer sections.

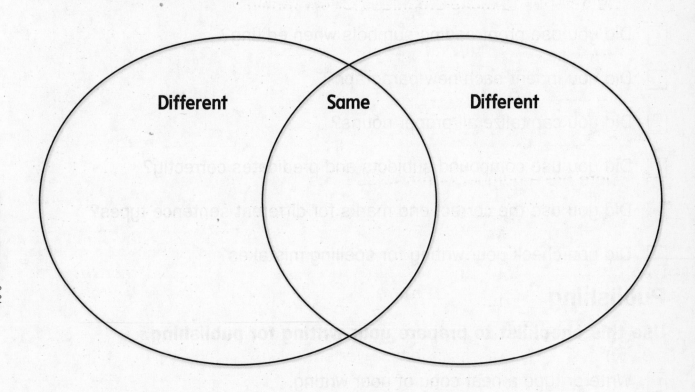

**Different**  **Same**  **Different**

# Revising

## Use this checklist to revise your writing.

☐ Did you include compare and contrast signal words?

☐ Did you include details and descriptions taken from the reading selection?

☐ Did you use your own words to describe the information?

☐ Did you include a concluding sentence?

☐ Does your writing have a clear purpose?

☐ Did you use a neutral point of view?

# Editing/Proofreading

## Use this checklist to correct mistakes in your writing.

☐ Did you use proofreading symbols when editing?

☐ Did you indent each new paragraph?

☐ Did you capitalize all proper nouns?

☐ Did you use compound subjects and predicates correctly?

☐ Did you use the correct end marks for different sentence types?

☐ Did you check your writing for spelling mistakes?

# Publishing

## Use this checklist to prepare your writing for publishing.

☐ Write or type a neat copy of your writing.

☐ Share your response to nonfiction with others.

# Spelling

> **FOCUS** A word changes meaning when a prefix is added to the beginning of the word.
>
> - The prefix *ex-* means "out of," "from," or "thoroughly."
> - The prefix *en-/em-* means "to cause or make."
> - The prefix *dis-* means "not."
> - The prefix *auto-* means "self."

**Word List**
√ 1. disprove
√ 2. expand
3. autopilot
4. employ
5. endanger
√ 6. distrust
√ 7. exact
8. automatic

9. empower
√ 10. extra
11. automobile
12. enact
√ 13. explode
√ 14. disband
15. enable

**Challenge Words**
1. disagree
2. autobiography
3. encourage

**PRACTICE** Sort the spelling words under the correct heading.

**Prefix *ex-***

1. extra
2. explode
3. exact
4. expand

**Prefix *dis-***

5. disband
6. disprove
7. distrust
8. disagree

**Prefix auto-**

9. Autopilot

10. Automatic

11. Automobile

12. Autography

**Prefix en-**

13. encourage

14. enable

15. endanger

16. enable

**Prefix em-**

17. empower

18. empty

# Past, Present, and Future Tense Verbs

**FOCUS** A **verb tense** tells whether the action is happening in the present, happened in the past, or will happen in the future.

Verbs in the **present tense** show what is happening *right now*, or what *always happens*.

**Example:** Monica <u>loves</u> the musical *My Fair Lady*. She <u>is singing</u> in the living room.

Add **-ed** to the present tense form of most verbs to show past tense. Not all verbs form the **past tense** by adding -ed.

**Example:** Phil <u>wrote</u> his report while his father <u>painted</u> the house.

The **future tense** is formed by using the helping verb *will*.

**Example:** People <u>will travel</u> to Mars someday.

**PRACTICE** Write *past*, *present*, or *future* to identify the tense of the boldfaced verb in each sentence.

1. I **will go** to Chicago this summer. _future_

2. Chicago **sits** next to Lake Michigan. _present_

3. A fire in 1871 **burned** much of the city. _past_

4. People **rebuilt** the city. _past_

5. I **will visit** museums there. _future_

**APPLY** Read the paragraph below. Circle verbs in the past tense. (Remember, not all of them end in *-ed*.)

On Saturday, we drove to the animal shelter. I immediately saw the perfect cat. He was an orange bundle of fur. "That's the one I want," I said. My parents weren't sure, but then I said, "I will take care of him. I will feed him every day." After the veterinarian gave the kitten shots, we took him home with us. I named him Tiger because of his orange stripes. "I am going to be a responsible owner," I told him.

**The writer of the passage below made some verb mistakes. Review the rules in the Focus box. Then, in each blank, write the correct tense of the underlined verb.**

When Emma Lin comes home from school, her mom <u>was</u> ✗

___is___ at work. Mrs. Lin always <u>left</u> _leaves_ a key for

Emma so she can get in the house.

One day, however, was different. Emma got home and saw that her

mom <u>forgets</u> _forgot_ to leave the key. Emma <u>is</u> _was_ not

scared. She thought to herself, "I <u>knew</u> _know_ what to do. I <u>went</u>

_will_ _go_ to the McCarthys' house next door. Mom

told me to ask them for help if I ever needed it."

# Location Prefixes

---

**FOCUS** A **prefix** is a word part added to the beginning
of a base word or root. **Location prefixes** are
prefixes that tell where something is located or
when something happened. Location prefixes
include **mid-, sub-, trans-,** and **inter-**.

- The prefix **mid-** means "middle."
  **midair** ("middle of the air")
- The prefix **sub-** means "under."
  **submarine** ("under the water")
- The prefix **trans-** means "across."
  **transistor** ("a device that controls the
  electronic flow across components")
- The prefix **inter-** means "among" or "between."
  **interlude** ("a break between events")

---

**PRACTICE** Add a location prefix to each base word or
root word so that the final word matches the definition.

1. ___Subway___ way ("an *under*ground transportation system")

2. ___transmit___ mit ("send *across* the airwaves")

3. ___midweek___ week ("the *middle* of the week")

4. ___interaction___ action ("a conversation or effect that happens *between* two people or things")

5. ___interrupt___ rupt ("to cause a break *between* a speaker's words")

**APPLY** Write the word from the word box that matches
each definition below.

| | | |
|---|---|---|
| midday | international | transit |
| transform | midsummer | suburbs |

6. Occurring between two or more countries _international_

7. In the middle of summer _midsummer_

8. The act of moving people or things across places _transit_

9. Towns or neighborhoods outside of urban areas _suburbs_

10. The middle of the day _midday_

11. To make a change in appearance or behavior _transform_

**Use words with prefixes from the Practice activity or the
activity above to write three sentences of your own.**

12. _____

_____

13. _____

_____

14. _____

_____

Word Analysis • *Skills Practice 2*

# Vocabulary

**FOCUS** Review the selection vocabulary words from "How Congress Works."

| | |
|---|---|
| current | interpret |
| debate | process |
| fairly | proposed |

**PRACTICE** Read each sentence. Circle the vocabulary word in parentheses that best completes the sentence.

1. Mrs. Takahashi took time to divide the treats (current/fairly) among the students.

2. Pay attention so you can follow the same (process/debate) as I do when trimming the dog's nails.

3. I hope you can (debate/interpret) these instructions, because they are written in another language.

4. The (current/fairly) residents of the apartment next door will be moving next month.

5. The cranky Rivera sisters seem to (interpret/debate) every little decision to be made.

6. The (proposed/process) law would increase funding for schools.

**APPLY** Read the sentences below. Answer each
question by explaining the definition in your own words.

7. Wendy thinks the game should be played <u>fairly</u>. How does she want
the game to be played? _____

_____

8. A professor has been brought in to <u>interpret</u> the ancient text. What
will the professor do? _____

_____

9. A <u>current</u> song is playing on the radio. How long ago was the song
recorded? _____

_____

10. Greg hoped that preparing dinner would not be a very long <u>process</u>.
What did Greg hope? _____

_____

11. Ming and his sister usually <u>debate</u> about which movie to see. What
do they do? _____

_____

12. Cora <u>proposed</u> that her team take a five-minute break. What did
Cora do?_____

_____

# Business Letter

## Think

**Audience: Who** will read your business letter?

_____

**Purpose: What** is your reason for writing a business letter?

_____

## Prewriting

Use this graphic organizer to plan your business letter.

| | |
|---|---|
| **1. Heading: Start with your address and the date.** | |
| **2. Inside Address: Add the name and address of the person to whom you are writing.** | |
| **3. Greeting: Start with _To Whom It May Concern_, or _Dear_ (person's name).** | |
| **4. Body: Make a request.** | |
| **5. Closing: End your letter with _Yours truly_, or _Sincerely_, and then sign your name.** | |

# Revising

**Use this checklist to revise your writing.**

☐ Is the reason for writing your letter clear?

☐ Did you make a request?

☐ Did you use precise words so the recipient clearly understands your request?

☐ Did you use formal language?

☐ Is your letter polite?

# Editing/Proofreading

**Use this checklist to correct mistakes in your writing.**

☐ Did you use correct verb tenses?

☐ Does every name begin with a capital letter?

☐ Is every word or special term spelled correctly?

☐ Does each sentence begin with a capital letter and end with the correct punctuation mark?

# Publishing

**Use this checklist to prepare your writing for publishing.**

☐ Write or type a neat copy of your letter.

☐ Sign your letter.

☐ Address an envelope to mail your letter.

# Spelling

> **FOCUS** A word's meaning can be partly determined by the meaning of its prefix.
>
> Some prefixes refer to number or quantity:
>
> - The prefix *uni-* means "one."
> - The prefix *bi-* means "two."
> - The prefix *tri-* means "three."
> - The prefix *multi-* means "more than one."
>
> Some prefixes refer to location:
>
> - The prefix *mid-* means "in the middle of."
> - The prefix *sub-* means "under" or "below."
> - The prefix *trans-* means "across" or "through."
> - The prefix *inter-* means "between."

**Word List**

1. transport
2. bifocal
3. uniform
4. midsummer
5. submerge
6. interrupt
7. tripod
8. triangle
9. submarine
10. multiply
11. multigrain
12. transfer
13. midweek
14. interstate
15. bicycle

**Challenge Words**

1. multimedia
2. interfere
3. trilogy

**PRACTICE** Sort the spelling words under the correct heading.

**Prefix *uni-***

1. _____

**Prefix *bi-***

2. _____

3. _____

**Prefix *tri-***

4. _____

5. _____

6. _____

**Prefix *multi-***

7. _____

8. _____

9. _____

**Prefix *mid-***

10. _____

11. _____

**Prefix *sub-***

12. _____

13. _____

**Prefix *trans-***

14. _____

15. _____

**Prefix *inter-***

16. _____

17. _____

18. _____

# Vocabulary

> **FOCUS** Review the selection vocabulary words from "The United States Capitol."

<table>
<tr><td>amateur</td><td>chamber</td><td>scarce</td></tr>
<tr><td>architecture</td><td>persevere</td><td>wing</td></tr>
</table>

**PRACTICE** Read each sentence. Then read the definition below it. Write *Yes* if the definition is correct for the underlined vocabulary word. Write *No* if it is not.

**1.** This <u>wing</u> of the house contains the living and dining rooms.

**part of a bird that allows it to fly** _____

**2.** The students crowded into the <u>chamber</u> to see the senators debate.

**a section of the heart** _____

**3.** Many cities in Italy are known for their amazing <u>architecture</u>.

**buildings or structures planned by an architect** _____

**4.** Even though Jim is only an <u>amateur</u> cook, his food is the best I've ever tasted.

**done for pleasure instead of a profession** _____

**5.** Hundreds of years ago, ice was <u>scarce</u> in the summer.

**difficult to get** _____

**6.** The questions at the end of the test were difficult, but Ann knew she had to <u>persevere</u> and finish.

**keep something so it doesn't spoil** _____

**APPLY** Read each sentence. Replace the underlined word with one of the vocabulary words in parentheses. Use context clues to help you. Write the vocabulary word on the line.

**7.** In the special match, <u>beginning</u> tennis players took on professional players. **(scarce, chamber, amateur)**

_____

**8.** The hot sun made it hard to <u>continue</u>, but Henry managed to cross the finish line. **(chamber, persevere, wing)**

_____

**9.** This <u>section</u> of the mansion was built just last year. **(wing, amateur, persevere)**

_____

**10.** After the senators left, the big <u>hall</u> was empty and quiet. **(architecture, amateur, chamber)**

_____

**11.** When food becomes <u>limited</u>, animals sometimes move to a different habitat to survive. **(chamber, scarce, wing)**

_____

**12.** When Joy saw all the familiar <u>buildings</u> around her, she knew she was close to home. **(architecture, persevere, chamber)**

_____

# Writing a Summary

## Think

**Audience: Who** will read your summary?

_____

_____

**Purpose: What** is your reason for writing a summary?

_____

_____

## Prewriting

**Use the graphic organizer to record notes for your summary.**

Topic: _____

| Subtopic: | Subtopic: | Subtopic: |
|---|---|---|
| | | |
| | | |
| | | |

Conclusion: _____

_____

# Revising

**Use this checklist to revise your writing.**

☐ Did you tell the main ideas and include additional details?

☐ Did you use your own words?

☐ Did you use time and order words to organize the sequence of events?

☐ Did you present a neutral point of view in the summary?

☐ Did you use formal language?

# Editing/Proofreading

**Use this checklist to correct mistakes in your writing.**

☐ Did you use prepositions and prepositional phrases correctly?

☐ Are all of your sentences complete?

☐ Is every word or special term spelled correctly?

☐ Does each sentence begin with a capital letter and end with the correct punctuation mark?

# Publishing

**Use this checklist to prepare your writing for publishing.**

☐ Write or type a neat copy of your summary.

☐ Include a visual element, such as a time line.

# Spelling

> *FOCUS*
> - Words that have the **same base word** belong to a word family. Adding prefixes, suffixes, or inflectional endings to a base word can change its meaning. For example, the words *liked, liking, disliked,* and *unlike* all share the base word *like.*
>
> - Synonyms have similar meanings, but one word's meaning might be stronger or more forceful than the other's. In this case, the two words have different **shades of meaning.**

**Word List**
1. knowledge
2. unlucky
3. director
4. chuckled
5. roared
6. direction
7. hurled
8. expandable
9. unknown
10. expansive
11. luckily
12. tossed
13. luckiest
14. directory
15. snickered

**Challenge Words**
1. knowingly
2. indirectly
3. overexpansion

*PRACTICE* Sort the spelling words under the correct heading.

**Words with different shades of meaning for *laughed***

1. _____

2. _____

3. _____

**Words with different shades of meaning for *threw***

4. _____

5. _____

# Words that share the base word *luck*.

6. _____

7. _____

8. _____

# Words that share the base word *direct*.

9. _____

10. _____

11. _____

12. _____

# Words that share the base word *expand*.

13. _____

14. _____

15. _____

# Words that share the base word *know*.

16. _____

17. _____

18. _____

# Prepositions and Prepositional Phrases

> **FOCUS** **Prepositions** show position or direction of a noun or pronoun.
>
> **Examples:** Throw the ball <u>to</u> me.
> Sparky jumped <u>over</u> the fence.
>
> **Prepositional phrases** begin with a preposition and end with a noun or pronoun.
>
> **Examples:** Throw the ball <u>to me</u>.
> Sparky jumped <u>over the fence</u>.

**PRACTICE** Circle the correct preposition in each sentence.

1. My grandfather bought this old coin (under / on) the Internet (for / by) twenty-five dollars.

2. The coin is (from / above) Europe.

3. The person who sold it (off / to) him sent the coin (in / before) a big padded envelope.

4. Greek letters are stamped (around / from) the edges (after / of) the coin.

5. Grandpa put the coin (at / in) a special frame and hung it (behind / on) the wall.

**APPLY** Read each sentence below. Circle the
prepositions, and underline the prepositional phrases.

6. The city of Rome is in Italy.

7. People have lived in that region for thousands of years.

8. Around 800 B.C., people called the Etruscans came from the east into northern Italy.

9. The influence of Etruscan culture can be seen in Rome.

10. People still find Etruscan objects buried under the city.

11. There are Etruscan tombs in hillsides outside Rome.

12. You can see Etruscan artifacts in museums.

**Use the lines below to write a paragraph with prepositions
and prepositional phrases. Circle the prepositions you use
and underline the prepositional phrases.**

_____

_____

_____

_____

_____

_____

_____

_____

Grammar • *Skills Practice 2*

# Prefixes and Suffixes

**FOCUS** A **prefix** is a word part added to the beginning of a base word or root. A **suffix** is a word part added to the end of a base word or root.

- Examine the following prefixes and their meanings:

  **oct-** ("eight") <u>oct</u>opus
  **cent-** ("one hundred") <u>cent</u>ipede
  **semi-** ("half" or "partly") <u>semi</u>tropical
  **para-** ("beside") <u>para</u>graph

- Examine the following suffixes and their meanings:

  **-dom** ("state or quality of") king<u>dom</u>
  **-ship** ("state or quality of") owner<u>ship</u>
  **-ent** ("inclined to") persist<u>ent</u>
  **-ous** ("full of") mysteri<u>ous</u>

**PRACTICE** Read each word below and circle the prefix or suffix.

1. hazard(ous)

2. author(ship)

3. (cent)imeter

4. deter(rent)

5. (semi)annual

6. (para)meter

7. (oct)ave

8. free(dom)

**APPLY** Draw a line to match each word below with its meaning.

9. parallel           **a.** full of curiosity

10. wisdom          **b.** existing next to

11. curious          **c.** a person between the ages of 80 and 89

12. octogenarian     **d.** inclined to be neglectful

13. centigrade       **e.** the quality of being wise

14. negligent        **f.** partly professional

15. companionship    **g.** a temperature scale ranging from 0 degrees to 100 degrees

16. semiprofessional   **h.** the state of having a companion, or friend

**Write two sentences that include words with prefixes or suffixes. Use words from either the Practice activity or the activity above.**

17. We have freedom whew we

_____

_____

18. _____

_____

_____

# Prefixes and Suffixes

> **FOCUS** A **prefix** is a word part added to the beginning of a base word or root. A **suffix** is a word part added to the end of a base word or root.
>
> - Examine the following prefixes and their meanings:
>   **post-** ("after") <u>post</u>graduate
>   **micro-** ("small, short") <u>micro</u>phone
>   **ir-** ("not") <u>ir</u>regular
>   **il-** ("not") <u>il</u>legal
> - Examine the following suffixes and their meanings:
>   **-ance/-ence** ("state or quality of") viol<u>ence</u>
>   **-ize** ("to make") energ<u>ize</u>
>   **-ist** ("one who does") biolog<u>ist</u>
>   **-ish** ("relating to") self<u>ish</u>

**PRACTICE** Read each definition. Write the matching word from the word box on the line.

| reluctance | English | finalize | postmodern |
|---|---|---|---|

1. The period *after* the modern time or era began _*postmodern*_

2. *Related to* England _*English*_

3. *The quality of* being reluctant _*reluctance*_

4. *To make* something final _*finalize*_

**APPLY** Complete each sentence by writing a word from the word box on the line. Use the definition in parentheses as a clue.

| | | | | |
|---|---|---|---|---|
| sluggish | postwar | capitalize | irresistible | guitarist |
| microphone | publicize | importance | dependence | extract |

**5.** Bree could not emphasize enough the _importance_ of doing research on the topic. ("*the quality of* being important")

**6.** The lead singer is using a _microphone_ so the audience can hear her. ("a device used to transmit sound or to make it louder")

**7.** Don't forgot to _capitalize_ the first word in a sentence. ("*to make* a capital letter")

**8.** The _postwar_ presidents upheld the treaty to ensure peace. ("the period *after* a war")

**9.** The company plans to _publicize_ its charitable work in the community. ("*to make* something publicly known)

**10.** In his rock band, Miguel is the singer and _guitarist_. ("*one who does* the playing of guitar")

**11.** Miners _extract_ precious stones from beneath the earth's surface. ("to pull minerals *outside* of the earth")

**12.** Jordan is feeling tired and _exract_ today. ("*related to* being inactive or unmotivated")

**13.** Petting the puppies was _____ for the children. ("not capable of being resisted")

**14.** Fawns outgrow their _____ on the mother deer over time. ("*the state of* being dependent")

Word Analysis • *Skills Practice 2*

# Vocabulary

> **FOCUS** Review the selection vocabulary words from "Marching with Aunt Susan."

| | | |
|---|---|---|
| appropriate | marched | ratify |
| campaign | mount | strenuous |
| factory | power | suffrage |
| liberty | rally | zeal |

**PRACTICE** Read each sentence. Think about the meaning of the underlined vocabulary word. Circle *True* if the sentence is true and *False* if it is not true.

**1.** Lifting a large rock is more <u>strenuous</u> than lifting a feather.

    **True**                         **False**

**2.** Women gained <u>suffrage</u> in the United States in 1920.

    **True**                         **False**

**3.** If you wanted to be alone, you could go to a <u>rally</u>.

    **True**                         **False**

**4.** Someone running a <u>campaign</u> has no interest in government or public service.

    **True**                         **False**

**5.** Cars are built in a <u>factory</u>.

    **True**                         **False**

**6.** If a group of people <u>marched</u>, they wandered slowly in all directions.

    **True**                         **False**

**7.** Someone seeking <u>liberty</u> wants to be controlled by others.

    **True**                            **False**

**8.** A puppy that plays with <u>zeal</u> is very active.

    **True**                            **False**

**9.** To ride a horse, you must first <u>mount</u> the animal.

    **True**                            **False**

**10.** Congress must <u>ratify</u> an amendment before it becomes law.

    **True**                            **False**

**11.** In a democracy, people have the <u>power</u> to choose their leaders.

    **True**                            **False**

**12.** It is <u>appropriate</u> to wear shorts and flip flops to a formal wedding.

    **True**                            **False**

***APPLY*** **Write the vocabulary word that best completes each sentence below.**

**13.** Boy Scouts _____ behind the band in the parade.

**14.** A successful _____ results in winning the election.

**15.** Avoid _____ exercise until your arm heals.

**16.** Women's fight for _____ lasted more than 100 years.

**17.** Council members voted to _____ the ban on smoking.

**18.** The United States gained _____ from England in 1776.

# Response to Literature

## Think

**Audience: Who** will read your response to literature?

_____

**Purpose: What** is your reason for writing?

_____

## Prewriting

**Use this graphic organizer to take notes about the character you have chosen from "Marching with Aunt Susan."**

| Character: |
|---|

↓

| |
|---|

↓

| |
|---|

↓

| |
|---|

↓

| |
|---|

↓

| |
|---|

# Revising

**Use this checklist to revise your writing.**

☐ Did you identify a main character in the story?

☐ Did you use cause-and-effect signal words to describe how events affect the character?

☐ Did you include details that describe the character's feelings and actions?

☐ Did you use language that is appropriate for your audience and purpose?

☐ Is your purpose for writing clear?

# Editing/Proofreading

**Use this checklist to correct mistakes in your writing.**

☐ Did you use quotation marks around any phrases that were taken directly from the story?

☐ Does every name begin with a capital letter?

☐ Is every word spelled correctly?

☐ Does each sentence begin with a capital letter and end with the correct punctuation mark?

# Publishing

**Use this checklist to prepare your writing for publishing.**

☐ Write or type a neat copy of your writing.

☐ Include an illustration of the character.

# Spelling

> **FOCUS** **Affixes** are suffixes and prefixes that are added to base words. They are their own syllables in words.
>
> They are used to change the meanings of words.

| **Word List** | | **Challenge Words** |
|---|---|---|
| **1.** renew | **9.** inactive | **1.** misquote |
| **2.** unpaid | **10.** blameless | **2.** distrustful |
| **3.** judgment | **11.** humidity | **3.** mythical |
| **4.** misbehave | **12.** collection | |
| **5.** biweekly | **13.** scientist | |
| **6.** midday | **14.** selfish | |
| **7.** assistance | **15.** leadership | |
| **8.** preview | | |

**PRACTICE** **Sort the spelling words under the correct heading.**

**Words with prefix only**

1. _____  4. _____

2. _____  5. _____

3. _____  6. _____

**List three base words from the spelling words above.**

_____  _____  _____

## Words with suffix only

7. _____

8. _____

9. _____

10. _____

11. _____

✗ 12. _____

13. _____

14. _____

15. _____

**List three base words from the spelling words above.**

_____  _____  _____

## Words with both a prefix and a suffix

16. _____

17. _____

18. _____

**List the base words from the spelling words above.**

_____  _____  _____

# The Great Migration

Big changes often start with someone's dreams. The Great Migration was a big change that made a huge impact on the United States. Over almost 70 years, nearly six million African Americans moved. Whole communities traveled from the South to northern cities. They dreamt of a better life. Their move changed our country.

Many people with different ideas met for the first time. In these new communities, fresh art and musical styles developed. Our country would not be the same without the many people who left home to follow their dreams.

In the 1900s, most African American communities were located in the South. But it was not an easy place for them to be. There was a lot of tension between different races. African Americans in the South were not treated the same as other people.

Some people wanted to make sure that this treatment stayed unequal. Southern governments set up laws to limit rights. These laws were unjust. Farms were also beginning to fail. The workers in the South depended on farms. Without them, they had no money.

It is no wonder so many African Americans wanted to leave. But the choice to leave your community is not always easy. The South is home to a rich heritage. This heritage includes food, music, language, and customs. These things are often the first things we think of when we think of home.

Migrating African Americans brought some of the best parts of the South with them. They moved to the North with great hope. They wanted more work, more money, and better places to live. They hoped for a better place in society. They believed that in the North, they would be treated fairly. They wanted equal justice.

And soon, the migrating African Americans began to find what they were looking for. They settled in communities that appealed to different talents. Many musicians went to Chicago. Chicago became known for its blues and jazz. Writers and artists found a strong community in Harlem, a part of New York City. Workers needing jobs turned to the industry of Detroit. Other cities developed thriving communities as well.

News of these new communities of African Americans spread back to the South. More and more people began to migrate north. It is easy to see the importance of the Great Migration. Those who moved north increased diversity in communities all over the country.

The success of these communities helped others stand up for their rights. Together, people began to push for civil rights.

The Great Migration spread dreams and ideas across the United States. It helped all people who were seeking a better life. African Americans faced many challenges. Yet they overcame them and set an example for others. They held on to their hopes and dreams. They carried them to their new communities, and they grew.

We can thank the people of the Great Migration for showing us that everyone should have an equal chance.

# Clothes for the Community

Clara stared into her closet. The gray day and the drumming of the rain against her window made her sluggish. With a sigh she selected something to wear.

As Clara rummaged through her clothes, she came to a sudden stop. She stepped back to survey her closet with a more critical eye and a smile spread across her face. Now filled with energy, Clara hurriedly got dressed and bounded down the stairs.

"Good morning, Clara," Mom greeted her. "Have you decided on a community service project for school yet?" she asked.

Clara grinned broadly, "Mom, I have the best idea ever!"

Mom smiled at Clara's enthusiasm. "Well, let's hear it!" she urged.

"You know that I have had a hard time deciding what to do," began Clara. "Well, I was just trying to find something to wear. I was staring at my closet, and I realized I have clothes that I never wear. Why not put them to good use? So, I decided that I want to organize a community clothing drive. Would you and Dad participate?"

"Of course," said Mom. "What do you have in mind?"

"We can go through our closets," said Clara. "We can donate to charity anything that is in good shape that we are not using."

Clara and Mom peered into the downstairs closet.

"Look at all this stuff!" said Clara.

They continued to explore closets throughout the house.

"Wow, this makes me realize how much I take for granted," said Clara.

"How so?" asked Mom.

"I always think I need more outfits to wear, but that is not true," said Clara. "Looking at all this stuff makes me realize how lucky I am. Many people in our community do not have basic necessities. It is my duty to share with them."

"That is a great attitude to have," said Mom.

"What if we include the whole neighborhood?" asked Clara. "That way we could get everyone involved in doing their duty."

"Sounds great," said Mom. "We can have people drop their donations here. We will plan it for a weekend so more people will be available."

"Maybe we can get the whole community together," Clara hoped.

They began sorting the items from the closets.

"I cannot wait for Dad to get home," said Clara. "He will be excited about this. I never knew how much fun it could be to help out our community," she continued. "I want to think of more ways to help others."

"Count me in!" said Mom.

# Vocabulary

**FOCUS** Review the selection vocabulary words from "So You Want to Be President?"

| | | |
|---|---|---|
| adversaries | interview | priority |
| ambassadors | pesky | slogan |
| anniversary | philosophy | spectators |
| execute | preferred | vain |

**PRACTICE** The underlined vocabulary word in each sentence does not belong. Cross out the incorrect word. Write the correct vocabulary word on the line.

1. The reporter badly wanted an <u>anniversary</u> with the football star.

   _____

2. If you are going to run for class president, you'll need a catchy <u>priority</u>.

   _____

3. Kim and Delia had a bitter fight and have been <u>ambassadors</u> ever since.

   _____

4. Of all the new foods she tried, Tia <u>execute</u> the chicken kebabs.

   _____

5. When the game ended, the <u>ambassadors</u> filed out of the stadium.

   _____

6. For his study of <u>spectators</u>, Wes read works by ancient Greek thinkers.

   _____

**7.** The camping trip was great except for those <u>vain</u> insects!

_____

**8.** Kyle is grounded until he makes schoolwork his top <u>slogan</u>.

_____

**APPLY** Read each statement below. Rewrite the sentence using a vocabulary word.

**9.** Many married couples exchange gifts on the yearly return of their wedding date.

_____

**10.** Our government has representatives in countries around the world.

_____

**11.** A complicated plan may be difficult to carry out.

_____

**12.** If someone is overly concerned with his appearance, he may not be attractive to others.

_____

**13.** Some basketball arenas have seats for thousands of people watching the games.

_____

**14.** A reporter might record a meeting she has with the president.

_____

# Making Inferences

---

**FOCUS** When you **make inferences**, you use text details and prior knowledge to conclude something that the author does not state directly. As you read an informational text, try to make inferences about the people, places, events, and ideas described. This will help you understand the selection better.

---

**PRACTICE** Read each paragraph. Use details in the paragraph and what you already know to make an inference. Write your inference as a complete sentence.

1. Jeff squeezed down the narrow aisle and found his seat. He threw his tote bag into the overhead compartment and sat down. Through the tiny window, Jeff saw workers loading bags and suitcases.

   **Inference:** _____

   _____

2. "Where did you come from, little guy?" Darcy asked. The puppy was shaking from the cold. Its black-and-white fur was matted and covered with mud. The young dog was shy at first, but then it crept up to Darcy and sniffed her hand.

   **Inference:** _____

   _____

3. Since the dam was taken down, the stream has begun to flow naturally again. Native plants have grown along its banks. Fish, birds, and other animals have returned to the area to feed and reproduce.

   **Inference:** _____

   _____

**APPLY** Use what you already know and details from "So You Want to Be President?" to make an inference about each president listed below. Write the inference, one text detail you used, and the page on which the detail is found.

**4.** George Bush

Inference: _____

_____

Text Detail: _____

_____

_____ Page Number: _____

**5.** Theodore Roosevelt

Inference: _____

_____

Text Detail: _____

_____

_____ Page Number: _____

**6.** William Taft

Inference: _____

_____

Text Detail: _____

_____

_____ Page Number: _____

# Compound Words, Antonyms, and Synonyms

**FOCUS**
- A **compound word** is one word that has two smaller words in it. Sometimes a compound word takes its meaning from the words that form it. Sometimes it has a new meaning.

  **shoe + lace = shoelace**  "a *lace* that is used to tie a *shoe*"

  **air + line = airline**  "air transportation company" (not "a *line* in the *air*")

An open compound is two separate words that are read together and have a single meaning.

  **vice president**  "a person who is second in command to the president"

**PRACTICE A** Circle the compound word in each sentence, and write a definition for the word. Use a dictionary if you need help.

**1.** Mom placed a scented candle in the candlestick.

_____

**2.** Our babysitter watched us for several hours after school.

_____

**3.** Jenessa mailed a letter at the post office.

_____

**4.** The birds begin chirping at the first sign of daylight.

_____

• **Antonyms** are words that have opposite meanings.
*Polite* and *rude* are antonyms.

• **Synonyms** are words with the same or nearly the same meaning.
*Polite* and *courteous* are synonyms.

A dictionary or thesaurus can help you find synonyms and antonyms.

## PRACTICE B Read each sentence below. Then answer the questions.

Miranda was *bothered* by the very loud music coming from her brother's room.

**5.** What are two synonyms for the word *bothered*?

_____          _____

**6.** Does the sentence have the same meaning if you replace *bothered* with either synonym?

_____

The jury will examine the evidence to determine whether the defendant is *guilty*.

**7.** What is an antonym for *guilty*? _____

**8.** Does the sentence have the same meaning if you replace *guilty* with the antonym?

_____

Word Analysis • *Skills Practice 2*

# Shades of Meaning, Regular and Irregular Plurals

**FOCUS**
- Words with different **shades of meaning** have nearly the same definitions. However, there are slight differences in their meanings. In a set of similar words, think about which word has the strongest or most powerful shade of meaning.

  Example: *big* → *large* → *enormous*

  *Large* suggests a greater size than *big*.
  *Enormous* suggests a greater size than *large*.

**PRACTICE A** Read the following sentences. Think about the meanings of the underlined words. Place these words in order from the least powerful to the most powerful shade of meaning.

1. Anya was <u>overjoyed</u> to see her friend from Russia.
   Devon was <u>happy</u> to represent his school at the spelling bee.
   Rachel is <u>content</u> reading a book on a rainy Saturday afternoon.

   _____    _____    _____

**Complete each series of words by writing a word that has the strongest shade of meaning. Choose a word from the box.**

| bizarre | filthy | sobbing |
|---------|--------|---------|

2. crying → weeping → _____

3. unusual → strange → _____

4. dirty → soiled → _____

# FOCUS

- To make many nouns plural, add the ending -s, -es, -ies, or -ves. These types of plurals are called regular plurals, because they follow certain rules. For example:

| | | | | |
|---|---|---|---|---|
| wind**o<u>w</u>** | + | **<u>s</u>** | = | wind**o<u>ws</u>** |
| be**a<u>ch</u>** | + | **<u>es</u>** | = | be**a<u>ches</u>** |
| territor**y** | – | **y** | + **<u>ies</u>** | = territor**<u>ies</u>** |
| thie**f** | – | **f** | + **<u>ves</u>** | = thie**<u>ves</u>** |

- Some plural nouns do not follow the regular pattern. These are called **irregular plurals**.

Some nouns, such as **salmon** and **moose**, have the same singular and plural forms.

Other nouns change their spelling in the plural form. For example, **woman** becomes **women**.

## PRACTICE B Write the regular plural noun form of each noun.

**5.** paintbrush _____

**6.** wolf _____

**7.** dream _____

**8.** factory _____

**Write the irregular plural form of each noun.**

**9.** fish _____

**10.** tooth _____

**11.** deer _____

**12.** child _____

**160** UNIT 6 • Lesson 1

Word Analysis • *Skills Practice 2*

Copyright © McGraw-Hill Education

# Vocabulary

> **FOCUS** Review the selection vocabulary words from "The Power of Music."

| | |
|---|---|
| archaeologists | lively |
| banquets | lyre |
| basis | Muses |
| endured | orchestras |
| entreated | palaces |
| humankind | remains |

## PRACTICE Write the vocabulary word that matches each example or description below.

**1.** feasts for a king   _____

**2.** begged for a new bike   _____

**3.** the Chicago and Cleveland Symphonies   _____

**4.** homes of ancient queens   _____

**5.** stones from a 1,000-year-old house   _____

**6.** all of the people in the world   _____

**7.** a Greek musician's instrument   _____

**8.** put up with a boring movie   _____

**9.** the goddesses Clio and Calliope   _____

**10.** a cheerful Irish jig, or dance   _____

**11.** people uncovering Roman artifacts          _____

**12.** trust or love in a friendship          _____

**APPLY** Read each sentence. Then answer each question
to explain the meaning of the underlined vocabulary word.

**13.** A team of <u>archaeologists</u> gathered at the site of the ancient city.
What were they probably doing? _____

_____

**14.** Changes in Earth's weather affect <u>humankind</u>. Whom do these
changes affect? _____

_____

**15.** A statue shows the Greek god Apollo playing the <u>lyre</u>. What kind of
instrument is he playing? _____

_____

**16.** Shelly <u>entreated</u> her friend to loan her money for a video game. What
did Shelly do? _____

_____

**17.** Pedro's aunt has played the cello in three different <u>orchestras</u>. Where
has Pedro's aunt played? _____

_____

**18.** Suzy and her friends played a <u>lively</u> game of tag in the backyard.
What was the game like? _____

_____

# Main Idea and Details

**FOCUS** Remember that the **main idea** of a paragraph or selection is the most important overall point that the author wants to make. The sentence in a paragraph that expresses the main idea is called the **topic sentence**. The author supports the main idea with **details**.

**PRACTICE** **Each paragraph below is missing a topic sentence. Read the paragraph. Decide what it is mostly about. Then write a sentence that expresses the main idea.**

1. _____

_____ Mozart could play the piano and the violin by the time he was five years old. It was around this time that he composed his first musical piece. While still a child, he performed for kings and queens in Europe. By the time he was 17, he was working as a musician.

2. It had not rained for several weeks. Fields were filled with small stalks of corn that were sagging and turning brown. Farmers could only look at this sad sight and shake their heads. _____

_____

3. _____

_____ Trumpets dating back to at least 1,000 B.C. have been found in Europe and Egypt. A certain region of Asia had trumpets even before that. And we know that people in Peru played trumpets as early as 300 A.D.

**APPLY** Identify the topic sentence and supporting details in several paragraphs from "The Power of Music." Record them below.

**4.** This paragraph is on page: _____

Topic Sentence: _____

_____

Supporting Details: _____

_____

_____

**5.** This paragraph is on page: _____

Topic Sentence: _____

_____

Supporting Details: _____

_____

_____

**6.** This paragraph is on page: _____

Topic Sentence: _____

_____

Supporting Details: _____

_____

_____

Access Complex Text • *Skills Practice 2*

# Writing a Limerick

## Think

**Audience: Who** will read your limerick?

_____

**Purpose: What** is your reason for writing a limerick?

_____

_____

## Prewriting
**Use this graphic organizer to plan your limerick.**

There was a _____ from _____  ***Rhyme A***

_____  ***Rhyme A***

_____  ***Rhyme B***

_____  ***Rhyme B***

_____  ***Rhyme A***

# Revising

**Use this checklist to revise your writing.**

☐ Does your poem meet your purpose for writing?

☐ Do the rhyming words at the ends of the lines follow the correct rhyming pattern for a limerick?

☐ Did you choose words that help create a silly or humorous mood?

☐ Do your lines have the appropriate rhythm, or sound pattern?

☐ Does your poem create mental pictures for the reader?

# Editing/Proofreading

**Use this checklist to correct mistakes in your writing.**

☐ Did you use correct spelling?

☐ Did you capitalize the first word of each line?

☐ Did you have a friend or another student read your poem to double check for errors?

# Publishing

**Use this checklist to prepare your writing for publishing.**

☐ Write or type a neat copy of your limerick.

☐ Practice reading your limerick out loud if you plan to give a presentation.

# Spelling

**FOCUS** This lesson reviews **compound words, antonyms and synonyms, shades of meaning,** and **regular and irregular plurals.**

**Word List**
1. wondered
2. calves
3. rubies
4. geese
5. weighty
6. washcloth
7. excited
8. arrive
9. series
10. knuckles
11. bored
12. heavy
13. suspected
14. depart
15. cookbook

**Challenge Words**
1. people
2. somebody
3. wristband

**PRACTICE** Sort the spelling words under the correct heading.

**Compound words**

1. _____

2. _____

3. _____

4. _____

**One pair of antonyms**

5. _____

6. _____

## A second pair of antonyms

7. _____

8. _____

## Synonyms with different shades of meaning for *thought*

9. _____

10. _____

## Another pair of synonyms

11. _____

12. _____

## Regular plurals

13. _____

14. _____

15. _____

## Irregular plurals

16. _____

17. _____

18. _____

# Nouns; Verbs and Verb Phrases; Subjects and Predicates; Complete Simple Sentences

> **FOCUS** **Nouns** name a person, place, thing, or idea.
> **Verbs** show the action, condition, or state of being of the subject. There are action verbs, linking verbs, and state-of-being verbs.
>
> A **verb phrase** is a verb with two or more words. The last verb in a verb phrase is the main verb. Helping verbs come before the main verb.

**PRACTICE A** **Read the story. Write *yes* if the underlined word is a noun. Write *no* if the underlined word is not a noun.**

The <u>story</u> _____ of the Frog Prince <u>teaches</u> _____ about honesty. The princess in the story promises a <u>frog</u> _____ he can live at the castle. At first, she does not <u>want</u> _____ to keep her promise. When she gives the frog a <u>kiss</u>, _____ he turns into a prince. By keeping her <u>promise</u>, _____ she saves the frog prince.

**Read each sentence. Circle *Action Verb* if the sentence has an action verb. Circle *Verb Phrase* if the sentence has a verb phrase.**

1. The girls danced to the music.          Action Verb          Verb Phrase

2. I dance, too.          Action Verb          Verb Phrase

3. I will go to school someday to become a dancer.          Action Verb          Verb Phrase

4. I will try hard to be a great dancer.          Action Verb          Verb Phrase

**FOCUS** The **subject** names who or what a sentence is about.

A **simple subject** is the main word or words in a sentence, usually a noun or pronoun. A **compound subject** has two or more subjects combined by a conjunction.

A **simple predicate** shows one thing about the subject. The predicate tells what the subject is or does. A **compound predicate** shows two or more things about the same subject. The verbs are connected by a conjunction.

A complete **simple sentence** has one subject and one predicate.

**PRACTICE B** **Decide if each sentence below has a simple or compound subject. Write *simple* or *compound*.**

**5.** Aesop told a story of an ant and a chrysalis. _____

**6.** An ant discovered a chrysalis. _____

**7.** The chrysalis was moving and swaying. _____

**8.** The ant and chrysalis became friends. _____

**Decide if each sentence below has a simple or compound predicate. Write *simple* or *compound*.**

**9.** The chrysalis did not say anything. _____

**10.** The ant walked by later and saw an empty chrysalis. _____

**11.** Overhead, a butterfly was fluttering and flying. _____

**12.** This is a well-known fable. _____

# Contractions, Possessives, Irregular Verbs, and Abstract Nouns

**FOCUS**
- A **contraction** is formed by combining two words. Some letters are left out when the words are joined. An apostrophe (') marks the spot where the letters were dropped.
  *he's* → *he + is*    *we'll* → *we + will*
- A **possessive noun** shows who or what owns or possesses something. To make a singular noun possessive, add apostrophe + -s ('s). To make a regular plural noun possessive, add an apostrophe after the -s (s').
  the *writer's* notebook    the *athletes' uniforms*

**PRACTICE A** Read each sentence below. Circle the two pairs of words in each sentence that can be made into contractions. Write the contractions on the line.

**1.** I (do not) think you have ever been to my house before.

___don't___

**2.** (We are) planning to leave, but there is a problem with our car.

___we're___

**Read each sentence below. Write the possessive form of the underlined word.**

**3.** We located the <u>hospital</u> entrance after walking around the building.

___hospital's___

**4.** Are all <u>judges</u> robes long and black? ___judges'___

**FOCUS** • **Irregular verbs** are verbs that do not follow a normal pattern. With **regular verbs**, the *-ed* ending is added to make the past tense.

Examples: ***jump*** (present), ***jumped*** (past)

Irregular verbs take on different forms in the past tense. They do not include the *-ed* ending.

Examples: ***make*** (present), ***made*** (past)
***think*** (present), ***thought*** (past)

• **Abstract nouns** name feelings or ideas. You cannot see, hear, smell, taste, or touch them. For example, ***sorrow*** and ***knowledge*** are abstract nouns. However, words such as ***brother*** and ***carrot*** are not abstract nouns, because they can be observed through the senses.

**PRACTICE B** Draw a line to match each present-tense irregular verb with its past-tense form.

5. sleep                    **a.** sent

6. lose                     **b.** left

7. leave                    **c.** slept

8. send                     **d.** lost

**Read each sentence below. Circle the abstract noun in the sentence. Underline any nouns that are not abstract.**

9. I was thankful for Mr. Sherman's generosity.

10. My sister has had much success making and selling her artwork.

11. Lily experienced jealousy when her friend got a new bike.

12. The book focuses on the romance of a young man and woman.

Word Analysis • *Skills Practice 2*

# Homophones, Homographs, and Multiple-Meaning Words

---

**FOCUS** **Homophones** are words that sound alike but have different spellings and different meanings. Think about the meaning of the word when spelling a homophone.

Example: **Weather** and **whether** are homophones.

The words sound alike: (we' thər)

But they have different meanings:

*weather* "the conditions of the atmosphere at any given time"

*whether* "suggesting a choice or possibility"

---

## PRACTICE A  Answer the questions below.

1. What is the meaning of the underlined word in the sentence below?

   A time of <u>mourning</u> is expected after a loved one dies.

   _Sadness/grief_

2. What is the meaning of the underlined word in the sentence below?

   In the <u>morning</u>, Remi eats breakfast with her family.

   _the start of the day._

3. Are *mourning* and *morning* homophones? Why or why not?

   _yes because they sound the same but have different spelling and meaning._

4. Use *mourning* or *morning* to correctly complete this sentence:

   Jenna and I went jogging at 9:00 this _morning_.

**FOCUS** **Homographs** and **multiple-meaning words** are words that share the same spelling but have different meanings and possibly different pronunciations. Homographs also have different origins.

| Homograph | Multiple-Meaning Word |
|---|---|
| ***minute*** | ***conduct*** |
| *mi' nət/mī nōōt'* | *kon' dəkt/kən dəkt'* |
| 1. "equal to 60 seconds" (from Old French) | 1. "the manner in which one behaves" |
| 2. "very small" (from Latin) | 2. "to lead or guide" |

**PRACTICE B** **Answer the questions below. Use a dictionary to determine the word meanings and origins.**

**5.** Sentence 1: Jada made sure the <u>content</u> in her paper was interesting.

Sentence 2: I am quite <u>content</u> reading a book on the beach.

What is the meaning and origin of *content* in Sentence 2?

To be happy /chill

**6.** Use the word *content* in a sentence of your own. Provide context clues about the word's meaning. I am content about the test.

**7.** The ocean's <u>current</u> is strong today, so I will not go swimming.

What is the definition of the multiple-meaning word *current* as it is used in the sentence above?

pull of the water.

**8.** What is another definition for the word *current*?

something happening rite now.

# Vocabulary

**FOCUS** Review the selection vocabulary words from "Little Melba and Her Big Trombone."

| | |
|---|---|
| beamed | melodic |
| blessing | rhythms |
| company | solo |
| composed | steady |
| daydreamed | thrill |
| discouraged | tilt |

**PRACTICE** Circle the vocabulary word that matches each sentence.

1. Amber imagined what it would be like to be an actress someday.

   composed     daydreamed     discouraged     beamed

2. In the middle of the song, Hector sings by himself for a minute.

   solo     tilt     company     daydreamed

3. Drummers in a band play regular patterns of beats.

   composed     discouraged     rhythms     blessing

4. Andy couldn't stop smiling after he won the spelling bee.

   beamed     melodic     company     blessing

5. Our soccer team feels sad and hopeless after losing another game.

   steady     discouraged     tilt     thrill

6. Daisy and her sisters spend time together at the park.

   rhythms     solo     company     composed

**APPLY** Write the vocabulary word that best completes
each sentence below.

7. Megan's parents gave their _____ when Megan told
them she wanted to go to college far away.

8. It was such a _____ to meet the star of my favorite
television show!

9. Mark played a series of notes on the piano that actually sounded
quite _____.

10. Mr. Carter _____ a song for the school choir to sing.

11. After the roller coaster zooms down the incline, it will
_____ us sharply to one side.

12. Tania's coach told her not to feel _____ when she
finished last in the race.

13. All through the night we heard the _____ drip of water
leaking from the faucet.

14. Lance doesn't know whether he is brave enough to sing the
_____ at the concert.

15. If you would like some _____, I will go to the mall
with you.

16. Grandma _____ at Stephanie as the little girl took her
first steps.

# Sequence

> **FOCUS** Remember that **sequence** is the order in which events take place in a text. Time and order words, such as *last week, March 5, 2008, first, before, next,* and *at last,* will help you identify the sequence.

**PRACTICE** Order these events from "Little Melba and Her Big Trombone" in the correct sequence. Write the correct number (1–10) on each line.

_____ Melba and her mother move to Los Angeles.

_____ Melba almost quits playing the trombone.

_____ Melba's mother buys her her first trombone.

_____ Melba plays with Billie Holiday's band.

_____ Melba plays her trombone for a Kansas City radio station.

_____ Melba is invited to tour with Gerald Wilson.

_____ Melba is born in Kansas City in 1926.

_____ Melba plays her trombone all around the world.

_____ Melba joins Alma Hightower's after-school music club.

_____ Melba teaches herself to play the trombone.

**APPLY** Write a paragraph that tells about your life so far. Include time and order words to make the sequence of events clear.

_____

_____

_____

_____

_____

Write a paragraph that retells the major events in one of your favorite stories. Include time and order words to make the sequence clear.

_____

_____

_____

_____

_____

Access Complex Text • *Skills Practice 2*

# Narrative Writing

## Think

**Audience: Who** will read your story?

_____

**Purpose: What** is your reason for writing a story?

_____

_____

## *PREWRITING* Use the story map below to plan how events will unfold in your story.

### Story Map

| Beginning: |
| --- |
|  |

↓

| Middle: |
| --- |
|  |

↓

| End: |
| --- |
|  |

# Revising

**Use this checklist to revise your writing.**

☐ Did you write a beginning that will grab the reader's attention?

☐ Do you include details about the characters, setting, and plot?

☐ Does the order of events make sense?

☐ Did you include realistic dialogue?

☐ Is it clear whether your story is realistic or fantasy?

# Editing/Proofreading

**Use this checklist to correct mistakes in your writing.**

☐ Did you use proofreading symbols when editing?

☐ Did you indent each new paragraph?

☐ Did you use quotation marks and commas correctly for dialogue?

☐ Did you use correct punctuation?

☐ Did you check your writing for spelling mistakes?

# Publishing

**Use this checklist to prepare your writing for publishing.**

☐ Write or type a neat copy of your story.

☐ Add a drawing or other illustration.

# Spelling

**FOCUS** This lesson reviews **contractions, possessives, irregular verbs, abstract nouns, homophones, homographs,** and **multiple-meaning words.**

**Word List**

| | | **Challenge Words** |
|---|---|---|
| **1.** we've | **9.** haven't | **1.** intelligence |
| **2.** chicken's | **10.** flower | **2.** information |
| **3.** your | **11.** brought | **3.** swallow |
| **4.** train | **12.** there | |
| **5.** talent | **13.** store | |
| **6.** students' | **14.** flour | |
| **7.** swept | **15.** you're | |
| **8.** minute | | |

**PRACTICE** Sort the spelling words under the correct heading. One word will be written twice.

**Contractions**

1. _____

2. _____

3. _____

**Singular possessive**

4. _____

**Plural possessive**

5. _____

**Possessive pronoun**

6. _____

**Irregular verbs**

7. _____

8. _____

## Abstract nouns

9. _____

10. _____

11. _____

## Homographs with the same pronunciation

12. _____

13. _____

14. _____

## Homograph with different pronunciations

15. _____

## Homophone pairs

16. _____ and _____

17. _____ and _____

## Homophone for *they're*

18. _____

# Possessive Nouns and Pronouns; Plural Nouns; Sentence Types; Subjects and Objects

**FOCUS** A **possessive noun** shows ownership. Add apostrophe + -s to singular nouns and plural nouns that do not end in s to form the possessive. Add only an apostrophe to plural nouns ending in s.
A **possessive pronoun** takes the place of a possessive noun.
**Plural nouns** name more than one person, place, thing, or idea. Add -s or -es to form the plural for most nouns. Irregular nouns do not follow this rule. You must learn their correct spellings.

**PRACTICE A** Rewrite each phrase using a possessive noun or pronoun.

1. the purse belonging to Angela _Angela's purse_

2. the hair belonging to the girl _the girl's hair_

3. the pen belonging to him _his pen_

4. the lids belonging to the dishes _dishes lids'_

**Circle the correct plural spelling from each pair of words.**

5. My mom tells **storys/stories** of when she was young.

6. Geraldo has two pet **mouses/mice** that are white.

7. Only an adult should use **matchs/matches** to light the candles.

8. How many **childs/children** will be attending the party?

> **FOCUS** A **declarative sentence** provides information and ends with a period. An **interrogative sentence** asks a question and ends with a question mark. An **exclamatory sentence** shows strong emotion and ends with an exclamation point. An **imperative sentence** gives a command or makes a request and ends with a period.
>
> The **subject** is who or what a sentence is about. A **direct object** receives the action of the subject. Subjects and direct objects can be nouns or pronouns.
>
> **Example:** <u>Jasper</u> ate some (treats).
> <u>He</u> ate (them).

## PRACTICE B Identify each sentence as declarative, interrogative, exclamatory, or imperative.

9. Have you heard the story about Demura? ___interrogative___

10. It is similar to the story of Cinderella. ___declarative___

11. Demura rocks a baby crocodile in a cradle! ___exclamatory___

12. Don't tell me how it ends. ___imperative___

## Read each sentence. Draw a line under the subject noun or pronoun, and circle the direct object noun.

13. A mother crocodile asks Demura to rock the baby.

14. She hands a lovely sarong to Demura.

15. Demura's stepmother and stepsister take the sarong.

16. The stepsister mistreats the baby crocodile.

# Inflectional Endings, Regular and Irregular Comparatives and Superlatives

> **FOCUS** • The **inflectional ending -ed** shows that an action has happened in the past. The **inflectional ending -ing** shows that an action is happening now or always happens.
>
> Examples: **admit → admit<u>ted</u>**
> **apply → appl<u>ied</u>**
> **plan → plan<u>ning</u>**
> **prove → prov<u>ing</u>**

## PRACTICE A Add an inflectional ending to change the underlined verb to the proper tense. Write the new verb.

1. Our teacher <u>supply</u> us with construction paper. _____

2. I will be <u>demonstrate</u> how to make a necklace. _____

3. Dexter is <u>carry</u> bags of groceries. _____

4. Evangelina <u>state</u>, "Please cross the street at the crosswalk."

   _____

5. Nina <u>regret</u> her words and apologized to Cal. _____

6. Water began <u>drip</u> from the rainspouts. _____

7. My doctor is <u>suggest</u> that I take a vitamin every day.

   _____

## FOCUS

- **Comparatives** compare two nouns or verbs. **Superlatives** compare three or more nouns or verbs. To make an adjective or adverb a comparative, add *er* for shorter words. Use the word *more* before some longer words.

  To make an adjective or adverb a superlative, add *-est* for shorter words. Use the word *most* before some longer adjectives and adverbs.

  Examples: **fast** → **fast<u>er</u>** → **fast<u>est</u>**

  **quietly** → <u>**more**</u> **quietly** → <u>**most**</u> **quietly**

- Some **comparatives** and **superlatives** are irregular. This means they do not follow the normal rules.

  *little* → *less* → *least*

## PRACTICE B Circle the correct regular comparative or superlative in each sentence.

**8.** Phillip is the (younger / youngest) of the four siblings.

**9.** Tara walked (more hurriedly / most hurriedly) than her Aunt Dawn.

**Write an irregular comparative or superlative from the box to complete each sentence.**

| worst | farthest | worse |
|-------|----------|-------|

**10.** Last winter we had the _____ snowstorm I've ever seen.

**11.** My dad had a bad cold, but mine was even _____.

**12.** Damon's last hike was the _____ he had ever gone.

Word Analysis • *Skills Practice 2*

# Content Words, Shades of Meaning, and Words with the Same Base

**FOCUS**
- **Content words** are specific to a topic or a subject area. Think about words that are related to the topic of government. For example, the word *legislature* means "elected officials who have the power to create or change laws."

- Words with **shades of meaning** are synonyms. However, there are slight differences in the strength of the words' meanings.

  Example: *cool* → *cold* → *freezing*

**PRACTICE A** In each set of words, circle two content words that are related to the topic of government. Write a definition for one of the content words.

1. damage        liberty        citizenship        temperature

_____

2. habitat        election        phrase        taxation

_____

**Read each pair of words below and think about the relationship between them. Use a thesaurus to locate a third word that has a stronger shade of meaning. Write the word on the line.**

3. amusing, funny, _____

4. sip, drink, _____

## FOCUS

- **Words with the same base** belong to a family of words. The base word itself does not have any prefixes, suffixes, or inflectional endings. Therefore, a base word can stand alone. When you add a prefix or suffix (or both) to the base word, the word's meaning changes. Sometimes, the part of speech changes as well.

  Example: **Base word** → *adjust* ("to change something in order to make it better")

  **Words with the same base as** *adjust* → <u>re</u>adjust, adjust<u>ment</u>, adjust<u>ing</u>

## PRACTICE B   Read each sentence. Circle the related word that can replace the underlined base word.

**5.** The elections were held in an <u>fair</u> manner.

   unfair          fairness          fairly

**6.** Our toaster <u>mystery</u> disappeared from the kitchen.

   mysterious       mysteriousness       mysteriously

**7.** He was rewarded for his good <u>behave</u>.

   misbehave       behavior          behaved

**8.** The president <u>claim</u>, "We must find a solution to this problem!"

   proclaimed       disclaim          claiming

**9.** If someone commits an <u>legal</u> act, he or she is tried in the court of law.

   illegal          legality          legalize

**10.** When traveling overseas, it is necessary to have proper <u>identify</u>.

   unidentified       identification       identified

# Vocabulary

---

**FOCUS** Review the selection vocabulary words from "Marshall's Role."

---

|          |               |
|----------|---------------|
| audition | harness       |
| flourish | opening night |
| glint    | props         |

**PRACTICE** Replace the underlined word or phrase in each sentence with one of the vocabulary words in parentheses. Write the correct vocabulary word on the line.

1. It is <u>the first night of our performance</u>, and the world will finally see our little play. **(flourish, opening night, audition)**

   _____

2. As sunlight sparkled on the water, the miner saw a <u>flash</u> of gold in the stream. **(glint, flourish, props)**

   _____

3. Before you can be in the band, you must <u>play a trial performance</u> for the director. **(flourish, harness, audition)**

   _____

4. The actors have to work with a number of <u>objects</u> during the play. **(props, glint, harness)**

   _____

**5.** The conductor signaled the beginning of the symphony by raising his baton with a <u>bold and sweeping gesture</u>.
**(opening night, flourish, audition)**

_____

**6.** A <u>device with straps and bands</u> connected Jon to a rope that allowed him to climb the steep cliff. **(harness, glint, props)**

_____

**APPLY Read the riddles below. Write the vocabulary word that best solves each riddle.**

**7.** I flash for an instant, like a twinkle in the eye. What am I?

_____

**8.** I am a tryout for an actor. What am I?

_____

**9.** I am a dramatic type of movement. What am I?

_____

**10.** If you have my ticket, you will see the first performance. What am I?

_____

**11.** I am objects that help a play seem realistic. What am I?

_____

**12.** My straps and bands can help you feel secure. What am I?

_____

Vocabulary • *Skills Practice 2*

# Fact and Opinion

> **FOCUS** Remember that a **fact** is a true statement that can be proven. An **opinion** is a statement of someone's feelings or beliefs that cannot be proven. Facts and opinions can be expressed by the characters and the narrator in a story.
>
> Recognizing facts and opinions in fiction can help you understand the characters and the theme of the story.

**PRACTICE** Write one fact or opinion about each topic. Use complete sentences.

**1.** the story of Peter Pan

**Fact:** _____

_____

**2.** your favorite movie

**Opinion:** _____

_____

**3.** classical music

**Opinion:** _____

_____

**4.** working backstage on a play

**Fact:** _____

_____

**APPLY** Explain whether each passage from "Marshall's Role" is a fact or an opinion. Use complete sentences.

5. "He was really good. It's too bad he's too young for the role."

_____

_____

_____

6. Marshall fashioned swords out of sturdy cardboard and glued silver glitter to the blades.

_____

_____

_____

7. Marshall backed off the stage as Peter spun around, and the swordfight began.

_____

_____

_____

8. "Thanks," Marshall said. "But that's okay. I really enjoy it back here with the sets and props. Besides, as far as I'm concerned, a backstage role is just as important as an onstage role."

_____

_____

_____

# Response to Literature

## Think

**Audience: Who** will read your response to literature?

_____

_____

**Purpose: What** is your reason for writing a response to literature?

_____

_____

## Prewriting
**Use this graphic organizer to order events in the plot.**

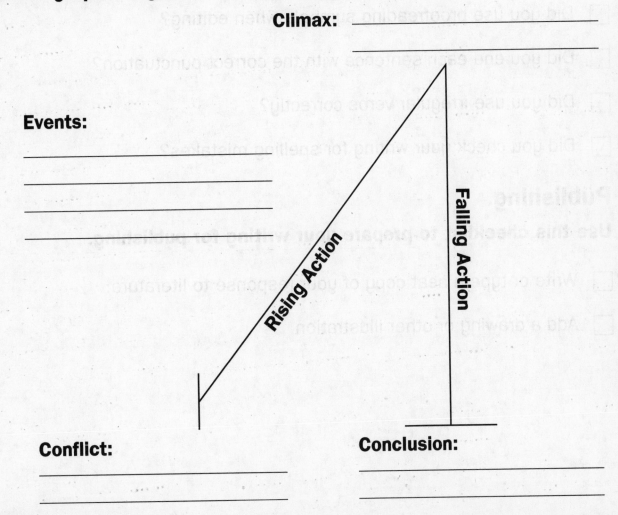

Climax: _____

Events:

_____

_____

_____

_____

Rising Action

Falling Action

Conflict:

_____

_____

Conclusion:

_____

_____

# Revising

## Use this checklist to revise your writing.

☐ Did you describe the important events in order?

☐ Did you include enough details in your descriptions?

☐ Did you use specific words and phrases to identify different elements of the plot?

☐ Did you use action verbs and descriptive words?

☐ Did you use time-order transition words?

# Editing/Proofreading

## Use this checklist to correct mistakes in your writing.

☐ Did you use proofreading symbols when editing?

☐ Did you end each sentence with the correct punctuation?

☐ Did you use irregular verbs correctly?

☐ Did you check your writing for spelling mistakes?

# Publishing

## Use this checklist to prepare your writing for publishing.

☐ Write or type a neat copy of your response to literature.

☐ Add a drawing or other illustration.

# Spelling

> **FOCUS** This lesson reviews **inflectional endings** *-ing* and *-ed, regular and irregular comparatives and superlatives, content words, shades of meaning,* and **words with the same base.**

## Word List

1. scour
2. chopped
3. least
4. sculptor
5. easel
6. departing
7. stronger
8. unpack
9. polish
10. gallery
11. stumbled
12. craving
13. greatest
14. packet
15. farthest

## Challenge Words

1. portrait
2. package
3. fancier

**PRACTICE** Sort the spelling words under the correct heading.

**Inflectional ending *-ing***

1. _____

2. _____

**Regular comparatives**

5. _____

6. _____

**Inflectional ending *-ed***

3. _____

4. _____

**Regular superlative**

7. _____

## Irregular superlatives

8. _____

9. _____

## Words with the same base

10. _____

11. _____

12. _____

## Words with different shades of meaning for *clean*

13. _____

14. _____

## Content words related to art

15. _____

16. _____

17. _____

18. _____

# Pronouns; Abstract Nouns; Conjunctions; Compound Sentences

**FOCUS** **Pronouns** replace nouns in sentences. Possessive pronouns replace possessive nouns. Using pronouns can make writing more interesting and less repetitive. Pronouns and possessive pronouns must agree in number and gender with the nouns they replace.

An **abstract** noun is something that you can't experience with your five senses. Abstract nouns name feelings, concepts, and ideas.

## PRACTICE A  Rewrite each sentence. Replace the underlined word or words in each sentence with a pronoun.

**1.** Josh, Mia, Ryan, and I worked on a school project.

_____

**2.** Michael scraped Michael's knee on the tree's bark.

_____

**3.** Mr. Johnston took care of my family's cat last week.

_____

## Underline the abstract noun in each sentence.

**4.** Your polite behavior at the restaurant is appreciated.

**5.** Please give me details about the concert.

## FOCUS

**Conjunctions** are joining or connecting words. **Coordinating conjunctions** join words or phrases. The most common coordinating conjunctions are *and, or, but,* and *so.* **Subordinating conjunctions** connect dependent and independent clauses. Some common subordinating conjunctions are *although, until, because, unless, since, if,* and *while.*

A simple sentence contains one simple or compound subject and one or more predicates. A **compound sentence** is made up of two or more simple sentences joined by a coordinating conjunction.

## PRACTICE B Underline the conjunction in each sentence. Then write *C* if it is a coordinating conjunction. Write *S* if it is a subordinating conjunction.

6. Jake or Missy will be staying with you this afternoon. _____

7. Until you feel better, you will need to rest in bed. _____

8. Jayden wanted to play catch with his dad, but he had to finish his homework first. _____

9. It is windy today because a storm front is moving in. _____

10. Chloe sat on the bench, and she sketched a nearby tree.
   _____

## Which of the sentences above are compound sentences? Write the numbers of the two compound sentences.

11. _____

12. _____

# Suffixes *-y, -ly, -ful, -less, -ion/-tion/-sion, -al* and Latin Suffixes *-ment, -ive, -ity, -able*

**FOCUS** • A **suffix** is a word part added to the end of a base word or root that changes its meaning. Some common suffixes include the following:

*-y* ("full of")   *-ful* ("full of")

*-ly* ("to do something in a certain way")   *-less* ("without" or "lacking")

*-ion/-tion/-sion* ("state of being")   *-al* ("relating to")

## PRACTICE A Write two words from the word box to complete each sentence below.

| | | | |
|---|---|---|---|
| appreciation | electrical | homeless | terribly |
| shady | meaningful | approval | powerful |

1. We wanted to do something _____ for the people at

   the _____ shelter.

2. Although the presentation went _____ wrong, our

   classmates showed _____ for our effort.

3. With their teacher's _____, the class read under a

   _____ tree on the warm, sunny day.

4. Last night, one _____ gust of wind knocked out our

   _____ system and left us in the dark.

• A **Latin suffix** is a word part derived from ancient Latin. It can be added to the end of a base word or root. Latin suffixes can change the meaning, part of speech, and spelling of base words. Some common Latin suffixes include the following:

-*ment* ("action of" or "process of")

-*ity* ("state of being")

-*ive* ("inclined to")

-*able* ("can be")

## PRACTICE B Correctly add the Latin suffix -*ment*, -*ive*, -*ity*, or -*able* to each base word to complete the sentence.

5. | humid + -*ity* | The _____ of the jungle made everything feel damp and sticky.

6. | inflate + -*able* | Children loved the _____ bouncy house at Grace's birthday party.

7. | assign + -*ment* | Rikki's homework _____ was to research the history of modern art.

8. | expense + -*ive* | Jewelry stores keep the most _____ items locked safely in a vault.

9. | judge + -*ment* | In my _____, homemade pasta dishes are better than those served in most restaurants.

10. | disrupt + -*ive* | The protestors were so _____ that the city council meeting was adjourned early.

Word Analysis • *Skills Practice 2*

# Multiple-Meaning Words, Suffixes -ness and -er, Content Words, Words with the Same Base, and Greek and Latin Roots

**FOCUS**
- **Multiple-meaning words** are words that share the same spellings and origins, but have different meanings and possibly different pronunciations.

- The suffix **-ness** means "state or quality of," and the suffix **-er** means "one who."

- **Content words** are specific to a topic or a subject area. Think about words that are related to the topic of weather. For example, the term **wind chill** means "a cooling effect caused by the wind, which makes the air temperature feel colder than it really is."

**PRACTICE A** Read the sentence below. Write a definition for each underlined word based on how it is used. Refer to a dictionary as needed. Then use your knowledge of the suffix -er to define the word with that ending.

The reporter wrote a <u>column</u> about the company's decision to <u>fire</u> two employees.

1. _____

2. _____

3. _____

Circle the weather-related content word in each set of words.

4. capital         poisonous         occupation         monsoon

5. octagon         atmosphere         independent         ancestor

## FOCUS
- **Words with the same base** belong to a family of words.
  Example: **Base word** → *consider*
  **Words with the same base** → *re<u>consider</u>, consider<u>ate</u>, consider<u>ing</u>*
- **Greek** and **Latin roots** are word parts that have certain meanings. Common roots include:

  *ast* ("star")      *graph* ("write")
  *log* ("word")      *scop* ("see")
  *mar* ("sea")       *grat* ("pleasing")
  *miss* ("send")     *port* ("carry")

## PRACTICE B  In each row, circle the words from the same word family. Then write the base word on the line.

**6.** substandard      standardize      statuette      _____

**7.** interruption      intensive      interrupted      _____

## Think about the Greek or Latin root in each word below. Draw a line to match each word with its definition.

**8.** marine            **a.** to tell people you are happy for them

**9.** autograph         **b.** a star-shaped symbol

**10.** congratulate     **c.** to carry something from one place to another

**11.** microscope       **d.** relating to the sea

**12.** transport        **e.** a special job a person is sent to complete

**13.** mission          **f.** a person's handwritten name

**14.** monologue        **g.** a speech in a play that is spoken by one person

**15.** asterisk         **h.** a tool used for looking at small things

# Vocabulary

> **FOCUS** Review the selection vocabulary words from "Behind the Scenes."

| coil | devices | loads |
|------|---------|-------|
| current | dim | physics |

**PRACTICE** Read each sentence and definition. Write *Yes* if the definition matches the way the underlined vocabulary word is used. Write *No* if it does not.

**1.** The theater lights <u>dim</u> for a second to signal the start of the show.

**become less bright** _____

**2.** Manny has studied <u>physics</u>, so he knows all about gravity.

**the science that deals with matter and energy** _____

**3.** The construction workers brought three <u>loads</u> of bricks to the site.

**things that are carried** _____

**4.** The scientists used several <u>devices</u> to run tests on the samples.

**thinks or makes up** _____

**5.** Electrical <u>current</u> can shock you, so be careful around those outlets.

**the flow of water** _____

**6.** In a speaker, a <u>coil</u> of wire is attracted to a magnet.

**a natural substance burned to make electricity** _____

# APPLY Read each statement below. Rewrite the sentence using a vocabulary word.

**7.** Frank hauled many batches of mulch with the wheelbarrow.

_____

_____

**8.** A technician replaced the speaker's broken spiral wire.

_____

_____

**9.** We turn down the lights when the baby is napping.

_____

_____

**10.** If the flow of electricity suddenly surges, power might shut off.

_____

_____

**11.** Janelle wants to study the science dealing with matter and energy in college.

_____

_____

**12.** Marco's lab is full of special equipment that he uses to conduct experiments.

_____

_____

Vocabulary • *Skills Practice 2*

# Cause and Effect

> **FOCUS** Remember that a **cause** is the reason why something happens, and an **effect** is what happens as a result. Look for signal words, such as *because, since, therefore,* and *so,* that will help you identify cause-and-effect relationships.

**PRACTICE** Read each sentence. Write *Cause* or *Effect* to classify the text that is underlined.

**1.** <u>When the noisy fireworks started</u>, Sasha covered her ears.

_____

**2.** <u>Mrs. Kirk is afraid of dogs</u> because she was bitten by one when she was a child.

_____

**3.** Stella is less than four feet tall; therefore, <u>she cannot ride on the roller coaster.</u>

_____

**4.** The tire on Zach's bike is flat, so <u>he'll have to walk to the park.</u>

_____

**5.** Many metals rust when <u>they are left out in the rain.</u>

_____

**6.** Since Nora cannot see, <u>her sense of hearing is better than average.</u>

_____

**APPLY** **Each sentence below is missing a cause or an effect. Write either a cause or an effect to complete the sentence.**

7. We packed our things and quickly left the beach house because

_____

8. _____

_____, so he has decided to start jogging every morning.

9. Since Justin does not brush his teeth regularly, _____

_____

10. Because this is the last day of school, _____

_____

**Read each sentence below from "Behind the Scenes." Write whether the underlined words describe a cause or an effect.**

11. When the weights on each side are equal, <u>the set or curtains stay put</u>.

_____

12. <u>The movement of the coil</u> causes the cone to move as well, which creates sound waves.

_____

13. <u>The flying gets more complicated</u> when the actor does twists, turns, and tumbles in the air.

_____

14. <u>Many theaters are very large.</u> People in the seats far from the stage could not hear the actors without help.

_____

# Biography

## Think

**Audience: Who** will read your biography?

_____

_____

**Purpose: What** is your reason for writing a biography?

_____

_____

## Prewriting

Use this graphic organizer to plan your biography. Identify your subject (person you are writing about), and list three details that you want to include about the person's life.

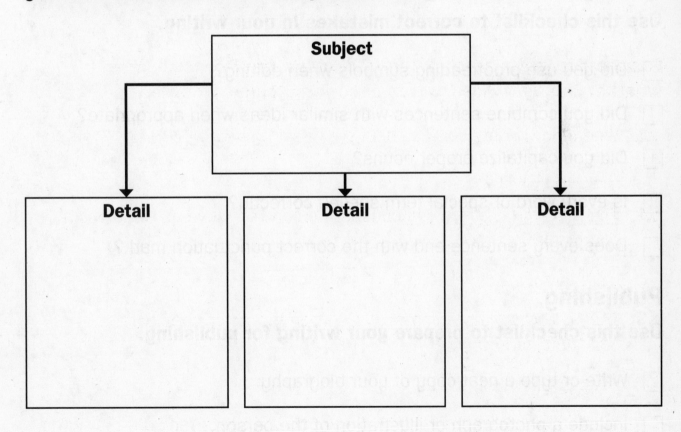

# Revising

**Use this checklist to revise your writing.**

☐ Did you include a topic sentence that clearly introduces the subject of your biography?

☐ Did you include interesting and relevant details from the person's life?

☐ Did you use time and order words?

☐ Did you include vivid descriptions?

☐ Does your writing communicate a clear purpose?

☐ Did you use formal language?

# Editing/Proofreading

**Use this checklist to correct mistakes in your writing.**

☐ Did you use proofreading symbols when editing?

☐ Did you combine sentences with similar ideas when appropriate?

☐ Did you capitalize proper nouns?

☐ Is every word or special term spelled correctly?

☐ Does every sentence end with the correct punctuation mark?

# Publishing

**Use this checklist to prepare your writing for publishing.**

☐ Write or type a neat copy of your biography.

☐ Include a photograph or illustration of the person.

# Spelling

**FOCUS** This lesson reviews the **suffixes -ly, -ful, -less, -ion/-tion/-sion, -ment, -ive, -ity, -able, -ness,** and **-er; content words;** and **Greek roots.**

**Word List**
1. trainer
2. monotone
3. positive
4. flawless
5. asteroid
6. quality
7. pollution
8. neatly
9. basement
10. shyness
11. invasion
12. solar
13. orbit
14. bendable
15. colorful

**Challenge Words**
1. monopolize
2. complication
3. affectionately

**PRACTICE** Sort the spelling words under the correct heading.

**Suffix -ly**

1. _____
2. _____

**Suffix -ment**

3. _____

**Suffix -ive**

4. _____

**Suffix -ful**

5. _____

**Suffix -less**

6. _____

## Suffix *-ity*

7. _____

## Suffix *-able*

8. _____

## Suffix *-ion/-tion/-sion*

9. _____

10. _____

11. _____

## Suffix *-ness*

12. _____

## Suffix *-er*

13. _____

## Content words related to space

14. _____

15. _____

16. _____

## Words with the Greek root *monos*

17. _____

18. _____

Spelling • *Skills Practice 2*

# Adjectives and Adverbs

> **FOCUS** An **adjective** describes a noun or pronoun, telling what kind, how many, or which one. **Comparative adjectives** compare two nouns. **Superlative adjectives** compare three or more nouns.

**PRACTICE A** Below is a folktale about Anansi the spider. The writer made some mistakes using comparative and superlative adjectives. Cross out any mistakes, and correct them. Underline the regular adjectives in the story.

One day, Anansi decided to take some food from the chief's farm. Anansi sneaked to the farm. He filled a huge bag with the most largest hazelnuts, walnuts, and almonds. The sneaky spider did not get caught!

Anansi kept going back. One night, one of the chief's loyal servants saw him. "This is the worsest thief!" the servant exclaimed. "I've got to catch him."

The servant made the shape of a man using the most stickiest rubber he could find. He put it near the beautifullest trees. When Anansi saw the rubber man in the darkness, he thought it was alive. Anansi yelled, screamed, and shouted at the pretend man. Anansi grew furious, and he kicked the man. His foot stuck! Anansi was caught!

**FOCUS** An **adverb** describes a verb, an adjective, or another adverb. Many adverbs end in *-ly*. Some adverbs compare actions. For short adverbs, add *-er* to form a **comparative adverb** and *-est* to form a **superlative adverb**. Adverbs ending in *-ly* use *more* and *most* to form comparatives and superlatives.

**PRACTICE B** **Read the sentence. Then answer the questions that follow.**

**The wind skipped quickly across the prairie today.**

1. What are the two adverbs in the sentence?

   _____   _____

2. Which adverb tells *when* something happened?

   _____

3. Which adverb tells *how* something happened?

   _____

**Underline the comparative or superlative adverb in each sentence.**

4. The sun shines brightest on clear days.

5. Neil walked more carefully after he tripped.

6. The painting crew arrived earlier than the plumbers.

# Prefixes *re-, pre-, mis-, un-, con-, in-/im-, ex-, en-/em-, dis-,* and *auto-*; Number Prefixes

> **FOCUS**  A **prefix** is a word part added to the beginning of a base word or root. Examine the following prefixes and their meanings:
>
> **re-** ("again")  **in-/im-** ("not")
>
> **pre-** ("before")  **ex-** ("out")
>
> **mis-** ("wrongly")  **en-/em-** ("in")
>
> **un-** ("opposite of")  **dis-** ("not")
>
> **con-** ("with")  **auto-** ("self")
>
> Examples: *restart, prewash, miscalculate, unafraid, converge, indestructible, expire, envision, dishonor, automobile*

## PRACTICE A  Circle two words in each sentence that contain a prefix presented in the Focus box above.

1. At my consultation, the doctor told me that I need to take some precautions to be healthier.

2. Aliyah was exempt from taking the pretest this week.

3. In her autobiography, the author mentions the injustices she dealt with as a young woman.

4. I am very disorganized, so I need to rethink my filing system.

5. Benson mishandled the situation by being unhelpful at a time when his friends needed him.

**FOCUS** **Number prefixes** are prefixes that indicate "how many." Examine the following prefixes and their meanings:

*uni-* ("one") *unison*    *tri-* ("three") *triathlon*

*bi-* ("two") *biannual*    *multi-* ("many") *multipart*

**PRACTICE B** **Draw a line to match each word with its definition.**

6. triplets      **a.** an animal with two feet

7. multipurpose      **b.** a shape with three sides and angles

8. triangle      **c.** to do many things at the same time

9. unicycle      **d.** having many different purposes

10. bilingual      **e.** three babies born at the same time

11. biped      **f.** to bring together as one

12. multitask      **g.** a vehicle with one wheel and pedals

13. unify      **h.** able to speak two languages

**Write a sentence using one of the words with a number prefix from the activity above.**

14. _____

_____

**Name** _____ **Date** _____

# Location Prefixes, Words with the Same Base, Shades of Meaning, and Prefixes and Suffixes

**FOCUS** • **Location prefixes** are prefixes that have to do with places or times. Examine the following prefixes and their meanings:

*mid-* ("middle")    *trans-* ("across")

*sub-* ("under")    *inter-* ("among" or "between")

• **Words with the same base** belong to a family of words. Example: **Base word** → *forgive*

Words with the same base as *forgive* → <u>un</u>forgive<u>able</u>, forgive<u>ness</u>, forgiv<u>ing</u>

**PRACTICE A** **Draw a line to match each word with its definition.**

1. transistor          **a.** the middle of the week

2. midweek            **b.** an underground train system

3. interject            **c.** a device that controls electronic flow

4. subway             **d.** to insert a comment into a conversation

**In each row, circle the words from the same word family. Then write the base word on the line.**

5. infection     reflecting     disinfect     _____

6. developed     delivery     undeliverable     _____

*Skills Practice 2* • Word Analysis                UNIT 6 • Lesson 5 **215**

**FOCUS** • Words with different **shades of meaning** are synonyms; however, there are slight differences in the strength of the words' meanings.

Example: *gully → ravine → canyon*

• **Prefixes** and **suffixes** are word parts added to base words and roots. Knowing the meanings of prefixes and suffixes can help you clarify the meaning of unfamiliar words.

**PRACTICE B** Circle two words in each sentence that contain a prefix or a suffix you have studied. Then look at each underlined word. Write a synonym with a different shade of meaning for the underlined word.

7. The semiprecious stone was made into a <u>glamorous</u> ring.

_____

8. The postgraduate was very efficient at completing <u>difficult</u> projects.

_____

9. Krista is a zoologist who <u>studies</u> insects such as beetles.

_____

10. Delete extraneous information when writing a <u>paper</u>.

_____

11. We took an introductory course on how to <u>gain</u> leadership qualities.

_____

12. I felt feverish after walking slowly across the <u>brutal</u> desert terrain.

_____

Word Analysis • *Skills Practice 2*

# Vocabulary

> **FOCUS** Review the selection vocabulary words from "A World Tour in Song and Dance."

| | |
|---|---|
| beat | rehearsal |
| commences | require |
| gestures | somber |
| inspire | specific |
| mimic | stressful |
| mourning | vary |

**PRACTICE** Circle the vocabulary word that best completes each sentence.

1. The constant rain and dark clouds gave us all a (mimic/somber) feeling.

2. Brad has been (mourning/commences) ever since his soccer team lost the championship game.

3. Lori thinks there is nothing more (stressful/specific) than speaking in public.

4. Actors should learn their lines before (require/rehearsal).

5. The beautiful scenery never fails to (vary/inspire) visiting artists.

6. Once the game (gestures/commences), you must call a timeout to stop the clock.

7. A mockingbird will (mimic/beat) the calls of other birds.

8. People around the world have different (gestures/commences) that mean "hello."

**9.** To make your writing more interesting, use (rehearse/specific) nouns and verbs.

**10.** You can use sticks or your hands to (inspire/beat) the drums.

**11.** Weather conditions (vary/somber) from one season to the next.

**12.** Tomato plants (require/somber) plenty of sunlight to live and grow.

## APPLY Read each pair of words. Write *S* if they are synonyms and *A* if they are antonyms.

**13.** beat            hit            _____

**14.** somber       joyful       _____

**15.** vary           differ        _____

**16.** stressful     relaxing     _____

**17.** commences   ends         _____

**18.** require       need         _____

**19.** mimic        imitate      _____

**20.** inspire       discourage   _____

**21.** specific      general      _____

**22.** gestures     movements   _____

**23.** rehearsal    practice     _____

**24.** mourning    grieving     _____

# Compare and Contrast

**FOCUS** Remember that when you **compare**, you tell how the people, places, things, or ideas you read about are alike. When you **contrast**, you tell how they are different.

You can compare and contrast things described in the same text or in two or more different texts.

**PRACTICE** **Read each sentence below. Write** *compare* **if it tells how things are alike and** *contrast* **if it tells how things are different. Then write what two things are being compared or contrasted.**

**1.** Hardly any vegetation can grow in either the desert or the tundra.

_____

**2.** Unlike his best friend Jacob, Connor is usually excited to try new things.

_____

**3.** A deciduous tree loses its leaves in the fall, while an evergreen has leaves throughout the year.

_____

**4.** Maria's apartment building is just as tall as the skyscraper next door.

_____

**5.** Blake prefers pancakes for breakfast, and so does his sister Bethany.

_____

**6.** I like playing the flute, but playing the drums is much more fun.

***APPLY*** **Answer each compare or contrast question below. Write a complete sentence.**

**7.** How are walking and skipping different? _____

_____

**8.** How are apples and oranges alike? _____

_____

**9.** How are bicycles and motorcycles alike? _____

_____

**10.** How are stories and poems different? _____

_____

**Compare and contrast traditions described in "A World Tour in Song and Dance." Answer each question below.**

**11.** How are dances in Hawaii similar to dances in India? _____

_____

**12.** How is karaoke different from performing with your own garage band? _____

_____

**13.** How are Khattak and Capoeira similar? _____

_____

**14.** How are New Orleans jazz funerals different from Tujia funerals of China? _____

_____

# Biography

## Prewriting

A timeline can help you organize the events of a person's life in chronological order. Use the chart below to record years and events. Then write the years and events in chronological order on the timeline.

| Year | Event |
|------|-------|
|      |       |
|      |       |
|      |       |
|      |       |
|      |       |
|      |       |

# Proofreading Symbols

¶    Indent the paragraph.

^    Add something.

℘    Take out something.

/    Make a small letter.

≡    Make a capital letter.

sp    Check spelling.

⊙    Add a period.

# Spelling

**FOCUS** This lesson reviews the **prefixes re-, pre-, mis-, un-, dis-;** number prefixes; location prefixes; suffixes; words with the same base; and shades of meaning.

| Word List | | Challenge Words |
|---|---|---|
| **1.** unreal | **9.** mistreat | **1.** interrogate |
| **2.** rewrite | **10.** biceps | **2.** meaningless |
| **3.** unwrap | **11.** midnight | **3.** interview |
| **4.** finalize | **12.** dislike | |
| **5.** wonderful | **13.** quartet | |
| **6.** finite | **14.** homeless | |
| **7.** question | **15.** finish | |
| **8.** precook | | |

**PRACTICE** Sort the spelling words under the correct heading.

**Prefix re-**

1. _____

**Prefix pre-**

2. _____

**Prefix mis-**

3. _____

**Prefix un-**

4. _____

5. _____

**Prefix dis-**

6. _____

**Number prefix *bi-***

7. _____

**Number prefix *quart-***

8. _____

**Location prefix *mid-***

9. _____

**Words with suffix *ful-* or *-less***

10. _____

11. _____

12. _____

**Words with the same base**

13. _____

14. _____

15. _____

**Words with different shades of meaning for *ask***

16. _____

17. _____

18. _____

# Subject/Verb Agreement; Commas; Capitalization

**FOCUS** A singular subject requires a singular verb, and a plural subject requires a plural verb.

- If the subject is singular, the present tense form of the verb usually ends in -s or -es.

- If the subject is plural, do not add anything to the verb to form the present tense.

- If the verb ends with a consonant and *y*, change the *y* to *i* and add -es to create the present tense.

- Some verbs are irregular; they do not follow the rules.

**PRACTICE A Choose the correct verb for each sentence and write it on the line.**

1. Roshawna _____ a storyteller. (are/is)

2. She and her sister _____ stories together. (tells/tell)

3. Last week, they _____ to a story festival. (went/goes)

4. Roshawna _____ a lot of fun. (have/had)

5. Next month they _____ a trip to Africa. (will take/are take)

6. Roshawna _____ it will be a great trip. (knows/know)

## FOCUS

The names of days, months, streets, cities, states, and countries are proper nouns. They must be **capitalized**. A **comma** is placed between the name of a city and the state or country. A comma is placed between the name of a day and month in a date.

**T**uesday, **M**arch 12      **A**tlanta, **G**eorgia
                               **N**orth **S**econd **A**venue

**Capitalize** the first word, last word, and all important words in the title of a book. For example: *No Room for Dessert*

Use **commas** to separate items in a list of three or more things.

## PRACTICE B  Draw three lines under letters that should be capitalized. Add commas where they are missing.

7. The festival will take place in st. louis missouri.

8. We will bring drinks napkins and silverware.

9. The date of the party is sunday april 23.

10. I love the book *the tale of despereaux*.

11. The book *cloudy with a chance of meatballs* is due back at the library on monday june 3.

12. On wednesday march 12, my grandma arrives home from dublin ireland.

# Art for Our Ancestors

Joe Kingbird's mom said, "You'll have a wonderful time, Joe."

"But you and Dad aren't even coming," Joe whined.

"What kind of attitude is that?" his mom replied, smiling. "Your grandfather is really looking forward to it. Besides, we have to travel for work; we couldn't go with you anyway."

Joe was not happy about visiting his grandfather. Especially since his friends were all at the beach.

It was a long drive to Grandfather's house. When they finally pulled in, Grandfather was waiting for them. As Joe got out of the car, he was shocked to see his grandfather. He wasn't dressed in his usual khaki pants and polo shirt; today he wore something *much* different.

"Hello, Joseph! We're going to a Powwow today!" his grandfather exclaimed. "That is why I am dressed this way." Joe did not know what a Powwow was, but if his grandfather wanted to go, it was probably boring and old-fashioned.

"Don't worry, I'll show you what it is," Grandfather said. "You should learn about your Native American heritage." They hopped in the car and headed out. By the time they arrived, it was already crowded.

"These people have come from all over the United States," Grandfather explained. "It's a way to honor our ancestors." As they approached a grassy area, Joe heard a deep drum.

"Can we watch the performance?" he asked.

"Yes," Grandfather said, "The singing has started already, so we should hurry."

Joe settled down on the grass to watch. To his surprise, Grandfather did not sit with him. Instead, he joined the line of singers. After waiting for his turn, he began to sing. His voice was clear and deep. After the song, Joe rushed to join Grandfather.

"I didn't know you could sing like that! It was beautiful!"

"Thank you," Grandfather said. "There are others with stronger voices. I just do it for enjoyment, and to honor our ancestors. Now, would you like to see the men's traditional dance?"

The two watched as men whirled and stomped to the rhythm. It was the most magnificent thing Joe had ever seen. When the dance ended, one of the dancers strolled over.

"Do you have time for me to show you a few steps?" the dancer asked.

"Sure!" Joe replied. The dancer went slowly, and Joe watched carefully so he could imitate the steps.

"Excellent, now you are ready," the dancer told Joe.

"Ready for what?" Joe asked.

"Ready to join us in the dance," the dancer answered. This made Joe nervous. He did not want to look silly next to the better dancers.

"The steps are symbolic," the dancer told him. "Visualize all those who came before you and think of a way to—"

"Honor our ancestors!" Joe finished.

"Exactly," said the dancer as the music began again. At first, Joe watched, but soon he whirled, twirled, and stomped with the rest. The drums excited him and made him proud.

"When is the next Powwow?" Joe asked as the music stopped.

"Soon, but what about the beach?" replied Grandfather.

"The beach can wait, but honoring our ancestors through song and dance can't!" Joe exclaimed.

# Martha Graham and Modern Dance

Martha Graham is known as a pioneer of modern dance. She brought her ideas to life on the American stage. She experimented with movement. She used to dance to express her feelings. Her dances featured sharp, jagged motions. They surprised viewers expecting the flowing, smooth ballet dances of the time.

At age twenty-two, Graham joined a famous dance school. Dancers usually begin when they are many years younger. But Martha Graham was anything but the usual dancer. She spent seven years with that dance company. There, she learned both American and world dance. Then she went solo.

Graham moved to New York City, where she developed her own style. The way the body moves had always interested Graham. Her father was a doctor and had observed movement to diagnose disorders. As a young athlete, Graham became aware of her own motions and movements.

She began to choreograph, or create, her own dances, as well as teach dance to others. At the Eastman School of Music, Graham directed the entire dance program. There, she could focus on experimenting instead of performing for others. She hoped to go beyond the fluid grace of ballet. Graham hoped to fill her dances with strong feeling and use her body to express emotion.

Graham taught her students different jerky, wobbly, and plunging movements. She used the pumping action of the heart as a guide for creating movement. She taught dancers to tighten and relax the body by breathing. Tightening caved in the stomach while at the same time rounding the back. Relaxing loosened the body and straightened the spine. These new ways to use energy freed the dancers she taught. They used her techniques to stir up emotion.

ke other modern artists, Graham focused her performances on just
...e basics. She did not use ornate props, sets, or costumes. She used
bare stages and lighting and wore simple dresses. She focused on the
movements instead of showiness. She wanted her strong movement to
express as much as the music she danced to.

Graham herself was a strong force. In 1936, she refused a request
to go to the Olympic Games in Berlin, Germany. At that time, the Nazi
party was in power. Many artists in that country had been treated
cruelly and unfairly. Graham did not want to be linked with a political
power that treated people that way.

Graham did not begin creating her dances with people or ideas; she
started with movement. She used dynamic motion to express herself.
Some critics thought Graham's dances were offensive. Her brand of
modern art shocked some. But Graham believed artistic change could
turn into social change. Her dances filled art with new energy.

Today, Martha Graham's dance company still performs many of her
181 dances. She hoped to be remembered as a dancer rather than
a choreographer. She felt that her heart belonged to being on center
stage. But in truth, she succeeded in both art forms. To this day, critics
compare her gift to that of important modern artists like Pablo Picasso.

# Vocabulary

> **FOCUS**  Review the selection vocabulary words from "Ah, Music!"

| accents | metronome | record |
| brilliant | mood | rituals |
| composition | primitive | universal |
| diverse | recital | variations |

**PRACTICE**  In each sentence, the underlined vocabulary word does not belong. Cross out the underlined word, and write the correct vocabulary word on the line.

**1.** Practicing with a <u>recital</u> will help you play songs at an even speed.

_____

**2.** The musician wrote his latest <u>mood</u> for a symphonic orchestra.

_____

**3.** Many composers wrote <u>accents</u> of the same tune.

_____

**4.** Fred knows a lot about the Native American <u>variations</u> practiced by his ancestors.

_____

**5.** I had to shield my eyes from the <u>diverse</u> light of the rising sun.

_____

**6.** Jake clapped for his sister at her dance <u>composition</u>.

_____

**7.** Maria woke up late and has been in a bad <u>record</u> ever since.

_____

**8.** There is a <u>brilliant</u> collection of many breeds of dogs at the shelter today.

_____

## APPLY Read the questions. Write your answers as complete sentences.

**9.** Can you tell when a musical piece has accents? Why or why not?

_____

_____

**10.** If a value is universal, is it held by people who live in different countries? Why or why not?

_____

_____

**11.** Could a new computer or smart phone be primitive? Why or why not?

_____

_____

**12.** Does a doctor's office keep a record of your health? Why or why not?

_____

_____

Vocabulary • _Skills Practice 2_

# Classify and Categorize

**FOCUS** Remember that classifying the information in a text can help you understand and remember it. When you **classify**, you sort objects or ideas into **categories**. Categories name groups of things that are related.

| reptile | paintbrush | oven | mammal | steel | palette |
|---------|-----------|------|--------|-------|---------|
| aluminum | refrigerator | easel | amphibian | dishwasher | copper |

**PRACTICE** Classify the items in the box. Write each one under the correct category.

**1.** Things an Artist Uses

_____

_____

_____

**3.** Kitchen Appliances

_____

_____

_____

**2.** Kinds of Metal

_____

_____

_____

**4.** Classes of Animals

_____

_____

_____

**APPLY** .......tioned in "Ah, Music!" by listing them under the correct category below.

**5.** Stringed Instruments

_____

_____

_____

**6.** Types of Singing Voices

_____

_____

_____

**7.** Kinds of Dance

_____

_____

_____

**8.** Instruments from Other Countries

_____

_____

_____

**9.** Percussion Instruments

_____

_____

_____

**10.** Musical Tempos

_____

_____

_____

**11.** Prehistoric Instruments

_____

_____

_____

**12.** Sections of the Orchestra

_____

_____

_____

Access Complex Text • **Skills Practice 2**